W9-DFL-417

NEW DIRECTIONS FOR HIGHER EDUCATION

Martin Kramer
EDITOR-IN-CHIEF

Building Robust Learning Environments in Undergraduate Science, Technology, Engineering, and Mathematics

Jeanne L. Narum
Project Kaleidoscope

Kate Conover
Project Kaleidoscope

EDITORS

Number 119, Fall 2002

JOSSEY-BASS
San Francisco

#56770964

BUILDING ROBUST LEARNING ENVIRONMENTS IN UNDERGRADUATE SCIENCE, TECHNOLOGY, ENGINEERING, AND MATHEMATICS
Jeanne L. Narum, Kate Conover (eds.)
New Directions for Higher Education, no. 119
Martin Kramer, Editor-in-Chief

Microfilm copies of issues and articles are available in 16mm and 35mm, as well as microfiche in 105mm, through University Microfilms Inc., 300 North Zeeb Road, Ann Arbor, Michigan 48106-1346.

New Directions for Higher Education is indexed in Current Index to Journals in Education (ERIC); Higher Education Abstracts.

ISSN 0271-0560   electronic ISSN 1536-0741   ISBN 0-7879-6332-1

NEW DIRECTIONS FOR HIGHER EDUCATION is part of The Jossey-Bass Higher and Adult Education Series and is published quarterly by Wiley Subscription Services, Inc., A Wiley Company, at Jossey-Bass, 989 Market Street, San Francisco, California 94103-1741. Periodicals postage paid at San Francisco, California, and at additional mailing offices. Postmaster: Send address changes to New Directions for Higher Education, Jossey-Bass, 989 Market Street, San Francisco, California 94103-1741

New Directions for Higher Education is indexed in Current Index to Journals in Education (ERIC); Higher Education Abstracts.

SUBSCRIPTIONS cost $60 for individuals and $131 for institutions, agencies, and libraries. See ordering information page at end of book.

EDITORIAL CORRESPONDENCE should be sent to the Editor-in-Chief, Martin Kramer, 2807 Shasta Road, Berkeley, California 94708-2011.

Cover photograph and random dot by Richard Blair/Color & Light © 1990.

Jossey-Bass Web address: www.josseybass.com

Printed in the United States of America on acid-free recycled paper containing at least 20 percent postconsumer waste.

CONTENTS

EDITORS' NOTES

Over 14 million students are enrolled in undergraduate programs in colleges and universities across the United States. Our goals as a democratic society can be met only if every one of these undergraduates has access to programs of the highest quality that prepare them for life and work in the world beyond the campus.

The premise of this volume is that the trustees, presidents, provosts, and deans responsible for shaping and securing the future of a particular college or university must commit to larger national objectives and translate them into action at the local level.

Today's world beyond the campus requires a new set of skills and sensibilities, a reality that is beginning to shape institutional transformation at colleges and universities across the country. A fundamental driver in such renewal efforts is the conviction that no citizen today can have a productive, self-fulfilled life without an educational experience designed to make him or her scientifically and quantitatively literate. Another conviction driving current institutional transformations is that the worlds of science and technology offer endless opportunities for students intent on pursuing a career in which they can make a difference. If grounding in the classics prepared leaders in colonial America, it is a solid preparation in science, technology, and mathematics that will help equip leaders for the twenty-first century.

To accomplish this for all undergraduate students will require a new social contract engaging everyone with a stake in a strong, vibrant society. This will be a costly endeavor requiring greater resources for investing in faculty, curriculum, facilities and instrumentation, new pedagogies, and technologies beyond those currently committed nationally or locally. It will require new partnerships within and beyond a single campus that collaborate in sharing ideas, insights, and materials that serve to strengthen student interest and learning in these fields. It will require time spent on individual campuses revisiting and reordering practices by which goals for student learning are set and met.

As a nation we must make a commitment, both philosophical and financial, to two objectives:

That all undergraduates in these early decades of the century have access to robust and engaging learning experiences that give them a deep understanding of the nature of science and of scientific process, alert them to the power and potential of science and technology in their world, make them facile with numbers and data and the use of technologies, and prepare them for responsible citizenship in a world dominated by science and technology

That each student, no matter the background, has access to a research-rich, discovery-based learning environment in which he or she is motivated to consider a career using scientific and technological capabilities, perhaps as a K–12 teacher, as an academic scientist or engineer, or part of the high-tech industrial community

There are several reasons for this imperative. One is that to be recognized today as an academic institution of excellence, a college or university must have robust, high-quality programs in science and mathematics. Applicants and their families seek such places; the retention of enrolled students in these institutions is high because students realize they can learn these fields and that this learning will make a difference in their lives. Those who make gifts and grants and those who seek employees ask for evidence that students are being well prepared for life and work in ways consistent with the institutional mission. Graduates, well equipped with the skills and capacities that leaders in this century need, become grateful alumni. This is a self-reinforcing process. But the fundamental reason is the historic American vision of an educational community that serves the larger national interest.

In addressing such objectives, decision makers in academe today must deal with challenges that are different in both magnitude and essence from those faced even as recently as twenty years ago: students are more diverse, resources are more limited, and the public is asking for greater accountability. But the single most significant difference between then and now is that the programs and spaces, policies and practices must serve all students.

When in earlier times, for example, the primary goal of a department of chemistry was to prepare students for graduate school, decisions about faculty, programs, budgets, and spaces could be made by members of that department with little consultation across campus. Presidents then took pride in the numbers and percentages of students admitted into prestigious graduate programs, and deans rewarded faculty and departments producing those results. Science and society were served.

This targeted approach had its roots in the national response to the *Sputnik* challenge in the early 1960s. The pressure then was to identify the best and the brightest students early in their college career and prepare them as quickly as possible as professional scientists and engineers. Courses were designed to filter for those best and brightest, and faculty interest in students was primarily to find apprentices for their research lab.

The strongest undergraduate programs in Science, Technology, Engineering, and Mathematics (STEM) fields today still have as a core mission to prepare those students who will be the next generation of professionals for the nation's scientific and engineering communities. Our society continues to have a desperate need for persons passionate about exploring, discovering, and designing at the frontiers of science and technology, people ready and well equipped to take the intellectual risks that lead to new understandings about the natural and the man-made world in the service of society. This need becomes even greater now as many *Sputnik*-era scientists reach retirement age.

But if academic leaders have agreed that the larger national objectives are relevant for their college or university, the process of planning becomes more complicated and more interesting. Decisions must be made from a wider perspective, including but going beyond how to serve a small cadre of students preparing for professional school.

It is precisely this expansion of the mission of undergraduate STEM programs that requires renewed campuswide attention to strengthening the learning environment in mathematics and the various fields of science, engineering, and technology. A commitment to make science a more visible part of the undergraduate experience for all students has implications for every decision to be made about programs and facilities that serve students in these fields, as well as the more general decisions in regard to policies for budgeting and for faculty review and reward. When the attention moves from the quality of teaching of a single faculty member to the quality of learning of all students, it becomes a community responsibility to make the right decisions.

Faculty with scholarly expertise in these fields must be actively engaged in shaping the future of programs for which they are responsible. The decisions made, however, will be more creative and more productive over the long term if they are the outcome of serious conversations involving each member of the community whose work can affect the character and quality of student learning on that campus. That decision-making groups are more productive and creative when they include persons with different experiences and responsibilities is well known to corporate leaders. Faculty informed about pedagogies such as collaborative learning are also familiar with the power of having diverse perspectives at the table in the process of identifying and solving problems. Trustees from the corporate communities can speak to expectations that graduates have the higher-level problem-solving skills, analytical competency, and technological sophistication needed to succeed in the workplace.

Think about decisions that must be made, based on challenges presented in the chapters in this volume:

• *The challenge of bringing advances in science into the learning environment.* In Chapter Seven, Diane Halpern challenges academic innovators to use in the shaping and reshaping of curricula and pedagogies what is known from research in cognitive science about how people learn. How can this become more than an isolated effort by a single faculty member? Is there a learning and teaching center, such as Susan Singer describes in Chapter Ten? Is there a team in place that links assessment of student learning to broader institutional goals, such as Christine Brooks Cote and Marianne Jordan address in Chapter Eight?

• *The challenge of expecting all students to succeed.* In Chapter Three, George Campbell challenges the community to expect that all students can learn in these fields and to put aside the sorting and tracking that has led to such dismal underrepresentation of persons of color in scientific, technical, or engineering fields. Is the campus community prepared to make the full-court press that the University of Texas El Paso has made, as Thomas Brady describes in Chapter Six, to build learning communities in which no student is left behind?

• *The challenge of nurturing faculty careers that serve new and persisting institutional objectives.* In Chapter Sixteen, James Gentile echoes the challenge in Chapter Nine from Project Kaleidoscope on investing in faculty: that someone on the campus take responsibility for knowing the needs and aspirations of faculty, individually and collectively, and for ensuring that those needs are met in a timely manner. Are institutional policies and practices in place that support faculty at each career stage and recognize and reward faculty for their contributions to strengthened student learning? Does each faculty member have a multiyear plan against which his or her scholarly achievements are measured?

Project Kaleidoscope is one of the leading advocates in the United States for building and sustaining strong programs in science, engineering, and mathematics. For more than a decade, its driving goals have been to equip teams of faculty and administrators for leadership in reform at the local level so that students and science are better served, as well as to encourage broad understanding of how strong undergraduate programs in these areas serve the national interest. To achieve these goals, the approach has been kaleidoscopic, giving attention to all facets of the undergraduate learning environment, from the quality of the faculty to the character of the facilities, from the design of the curriculum to the shape of the institutional culture and budgets.

• *The challenge of making the right capital investments in facilities and technologies.* Several chapters, in particular those by Arthur Lidsky (Chapter Twelve) and David McArthur (Chapter Thirteen), address the challenge of starting from the point of the institutional mission as decisions about major capital expenditures are being made. For many colleges and universities, a new or renovated facility for science is the largest investment made in decades in the physical plant; for all institutions, the constant demand for state-of-the-art technologies is requiring heavy financial commitments in the short and long terms. What are the goals for student learning that shape decisions about facility location or traffic patterns to and through a new facility? Are spaces designed to accommodate active learning communities and a research-active faculty and student body? Is the planning strategic or random for infusing technologies into the environment for learning?

• *The challenge to take bold steps.* Daniel Sullivan in Chapter Fourteen and James Appleton in Chapter Seventeen suggest that the transformation of these programs must be in the president's heart as well as in his or her head. Their counsel is that the more that the president and other senior decision makers are science-savvy, the better they will be in imagining and realizing objectives that strengthen the reputation of the college or university as one truly meeting the needs of students, science, and society.

There are more challenges, explicit and implied, in the chapters in this book. Collectively, they challenge academic leaders to take immediate and informed action. There is an urgency with the growing national need for a well-equipped talent pool from which the scientific, technical, and engineering workforce in the twenty-first century will be drawn. Today's undergraduates are that talent pool, and decisions made at the local and national levels about the quality and character of the learning that each student experiences will shape the quality and character of the national talent pool for decades to come. These decisions will shape the future of education at the K–12 level, as well as the capacity of the United States to sustain global leadership in exploring new scientific and technological worlds.

In a festschrift (1960) in memory of President Woodrow Wilson, poet Archibald MacLeish used the words of noted educator and public servant, James Bryant Conant: "What [President] Wilson meant by the wholly awakened person who should be the ideal product of American higher education is a person awakened through the power of the imagination to a consciousness of possibilities" (p. 7). MacLeish explains that "Conant assures us that scientific discovery begins not in the finding of the laboratory but in the glimpses of the imagination. . . . that the true scientist takes off, as the true poet does, not from the notes on his desk, but from a hunch, a feel in the bones, in intimation. If that is true, Mr. Wilson's whole person will make the better scientist, as he or she will be the better citizen of a free nation" (p. 8).

Reference

MacLeish, A. "Mr. Wilson and the Nation's Need." In Woodrow Wilson Foundation, *Education in the Nation's Service: A Series of Essays on American Education Today*. New York: Praeger, 1960.

Jeanne L. Narum
Kate Conover
Editors

JEANNE L. NARUM is director of Project Kaleidoscope and the Independent Colleges Office, Washington, D.C.

KATE CONOVER is writer-editor at Project Kaleidoscope and an assistant editor at the Journal of Politics and the Life Sciences.

PART ONE

Social Demands and Student Needs

1

Today's challenges, like those of the Sputnik era almost
fifty years ago, require a visible and persistent national
commitment to educational renewal and reform.

The National Context for Reform

G. Doyle Daves, Jr.

For more than a decade, perceptive leaders have been calling for a reevaluation of the priorities and practices of America's institutions of higher learning. Much of this attention has focused on those parts of the enterprise that deal with science, mathematics, and engineering, with attention to technology surfacing more recently. Some may find it surprising that those calling for educational reform would focus here, for in most colleges and universities, these disciplines, perhaps more than others, have thrived in the post–World War II (post-*Sputnik*) era. Indeed, the graduates who have poured out of our colleges and universities in the past fifty years with majors in these fields have literally changed our society in ways that have allowed more people to live longer, healthier, more fulfilling lives than at any previous time in history.

Why, then, the call for reforms? There are a number of concerns. One is the sheer size of contemporary academic science and engineering in the United States. Many in government have worried that the national scientific enterprise is growing beyond the point of sustainability. And indeed it has grown enormously. As recently as 1955, only eleven American universities had research expenditures of $5 million or more. Today, even adjusting for inflation, over 150 universities exceed that. In 1963, de Solla Price reported that world scientific output, however measured, has doubled approximately every fifteen years for at least three centuries, noting even then that this exponential growth could not be sustained indefinitely. In the nearly four decades since that report, the scientific research enterprise has again doubled twice, continuing the trend. Today, the investment of research in the United States is between 2 and 3 percent of gross domestic product (GDP). One might imagine one more doubling to about 5 percent of GDP, but surely our society will not support significant increase beyond that. This situation has led British scholar John Ziman (1994) to argue that the long period of dramatic growth in scientific research (at least in developed countries) has essentially reached its limit and that we are now in a dynamic steady state. He suggests that we have entered into a permanent climate of extreme resource scarcity for science.

A second concern that has led to calls for reform of academic science is the sense that for too many years, our research universities, and to a surprising extent our four-year colleges and comprehensive universities also, have focused on faculty research to the detriment of student learning. David Goodstein (1993), president of California Institute of Technology, has put it bluntly: "We have the finest scientists in the world, and we also have the worst science education in the world. Science education [here] is like a mining and sorting operation, designed to cast aside most of the mass of common human debris, but at the same time to discover and rescue diamonds in the rough" (p. 61).

From serious review of our nation's higher education community, a sobering picture has emerged. We see an enterprise geared to conducting research and sustaining itself by recruiting from among the large numbers of students who pass through our campuses only those select few who could be developed into the next generation of scientists. This focus has understandably worried leaders who think more broadly about the needs of society. Let me be clear: this is not a concern that the quality and numbers of students pursuing advanced degrees and careers in these fields is too high. We have an enduring national interest in the character of the talent pool from which comes the next generation of discoverers and designers for America's research and development communities, within and beyond academe. However, there is a growing national awareness that more must be expected from undergraduate colleges and universities.

Thus, there is another concern, a growing one, with leaders from public life, business, and industry calling for deep reform of education programs in fields related to STEM. Until recently, a working premise on which national decisions have been made is that our society required a relatively small percentage of white-collar workers, say 15 percent, and a much larger number of blue-collar workers. (Most educators have assumed that this division represented pretty accurately the innate distribution of capabilities of the human population to learn at advanced levels.)

However, our society is changing rapidly, placing new demands on the workforce. Fewer and fewer jobs are unaffected by the high-tech revolution. Recently introduced legislation in both the House and the Senate would provide support for activities that increase the number of majors in the information and physical sciences. At the minimum, everyone needs good communication and numeracy skills to succeed where they work and in their role as citizens.

An educational culture designed to prepare only the 15 percent of potential white-collar workers is no longer adequate. Neither is an undergraduate curriculum designed primarily to prepare the next generation of rocket scientists or Nobel laureates. Increasingly, it is the province of leaders of colleges and universities to ensure that each of their undergraduates leaves well equipped with the skills needed for success in life. It is equally imperative that those making decisions about institutional aims and objectives consider the role and responsibility of their institution in preparing the K–12 teachers now needed in the nation's elementary and secondary schools. Others too have made a compelling argument in this regard.

These concerns and the corresponding incentives for reform of the academic STEM educational enterprise have been increasingly evident in the past fifteen or more years. And as Project Kaleidoscope has so effectively demonstrated, the number of institutions and the number of faculty involved in the improvement of scientific, technological, and quantitative education has grown dramatically. That educational cultures can be changed to strengthen the learning of all students is clear from many demonstration projects on campuses across the country, as well as from both fundamental and applied research. We know that the quality of learning is a function of the quality of the learning environment, and that when proper learning environments are provided—no easy task—most people can and will learn effectively. But although there are now many institutions that have made and sustained impressive commitments to the improvement of learning environments for students, honesty requires an acknowledgment that no research university and relatively few institutions in other sectors of higher education have come close to the goal of providing truly effective learning environments for all students.

To understand how we might bring about and sustain such a reform, it is useful for academic leaders to look back. A great change in American higher education occurred in the decades following World War II. Much of this change was very positive and has been and will be indefinitely sustained. How did this happen?

The highly visible contributions of science and engineering to the Allied success in World War II—the atomic bomb, radar, penicillin—raised public consciousness of science and increased support for public funding of research. This new national commitment to research was epitomized by Vannevar Bush's 1945 report to President Truman, *Science—The Endless Frontier,* which led to the formation of the National Science Foundation. Symbolically at least, this report established a social contract between the government and universities for the support of research and graduate education. This government commitment had great consequences. Funding for university research increased sevenfold in the decade from 1958 to 1968. This enormous and sustained infusion of money is what brought about the focus on and great increase in academic research and, I think, as an unintended consequence, the lessening of attention to the education of the general student body. Today, essentially all science and engineering faculty members came of age in this period in which most rewards for both faculty and academic institutions themselves were a direct consequence of the commitment to research, an age so unlike that of the previous era.

It is important to remember that the change from a primarily teaching institution to one devoted to research was not accomplished without great pain on the part of many. At the beginning of the transition many decades ago, most faculty members were ill equipped for the new challenge and often not inclined to make the change. Many new faculty, hired to build research programs, tended to view the carry-over faculty as "dead wood" to be shunted aside as much as possible and as soon as possible. Over time, the faculty body changed to include a majority with individual commitments to personal research programs; this profile has endured because funding for research and reward systems for both institutions and faculty have strongly reinforced this pattern. To a lesser degree, this progression to a much more research-centered profile has also penetrated the comprehensive universities and liberal arts colleges. After all, their faculties and much of the academic value system originate in the research universities.

To achieve an American academy with strong programs in STEM fields—with an effective, sustainable balance between scholarship and research and a corresponding commitment to providing rich learning environments that foster the intellectual growth of all undergraduate students— will require serious change. While most see academia as having great inertia and ability to resist outside pressures for such major change, the dramatic postwar transition that created our research-centric institutions effectively demonstrates how quickly change can occur when conditions are favorable. There is a lesson in this for the efforts to bring American higher education more in line with the needs of our contemporary high-tech, multicultural global society. Society must reward, and continue to reward, the institutional characteristics that it truly values. In the United States, the most effective mechanism to make this societal will manifest is through government funding and regulation. This is what has worked so effectively in fostering faculty research in institutions of higher education.

The pressures on academia for reform are great and growing. As early as 1994, Charles M. Vest, president of MIT, alerted the community: "For half a century, federal agencies have funded research and graduate education programs that have been uncommonly successful. Nonetheless, the public and Congress now increasingly question the value, priority and relevance of this investment. The sense of partnership between government and universities has decayed dramatically."

The social contract between government (that is, the American public) and higher education institutions established in the 1950s must be renegotiated. For American higher education to serve the nation in the coming decades as effectively as it has served in previous eras will require a new articulation and understanding of the fundamental mission. This must include a clear commitment to help each student reach his or her individual potential by the development of intellectual, cultural, conceptual, communication, numeric and independent reasoning, and evaluation skills. Faculty, students, and society at large must understand and agree that the development of these personal traits, not the mastery of specific subject matter, is the goal of an effective college education.

Most curricula and pedagogy in the undergraduate arena are ill suited to the achievement of these goals. We remain largely focused on sorting and identifying the select few already destined to become professionals. A significant majority of college graduates leave campus poorly equipped for the challenge of effective participation in our increasingly complex technological society. Agreement on clear expectations for students attending our institutions can provide the basis for a new social contract that recognizes that great change will be required and support must be available, on a continuing basis, for the institutions and faculty who must bring about the change.

Currently, agencies, governmental and private, that support educational development at the undergraduate level see their roles as providing seed funding to try new ideas or to begin change, primarily through support for individual investigators or faculty scholars. They then expect institutional funding to take over and sustain the resulting programs. This is not realistic. Deep, systemic change takes sustained effort by seasoned professionals who continue to innovate, learn, and disseminate results, with the full commitment of their college or university behind them. All too often, seed funding allows an effective team to be assembled and begin to make important progress just as funding is exhausted. Like other research and development, systemic redevelopment of the educational enterprise is incremental and requires entire faculties to master new concepts and practices. It also requires the continual initiation of new recruits just as we do through graduate and postdoctoral programs in science and engineering. National leaders who are calling for change must recognize these needs and help create effective policies to address them.

The priorities of our society are demonstrated by what receives sustained funding (public, private, and institutional) and what leads to other forms of tangible support. What is rewarded is what gets accomplished. We must agree on what we want American higher education to accomplish and provide the sustained support that will allow it to be done. This will require a collective effort if we are to achieve an undergraduate learning community that truly serves the national interest.

References

Bush, V. *Science—The Endless Frontier*. Washington, D.C.: U.S. Government Printing Office, 1945.

Goodstein, D. "Scientific Elites and Scientific Illiterates." In *Proceedings of a Forum on Ethics, Values, and the Promise of Science.* Research Triangle Park, N.C.: Sigma Xi, 1993.

de Solla Price, D. *Little Science, Big Science.* New York: Columbia University Press, 1963.

Vest, C. M. *Annual Report to the MIT Community.* [http://web.mit.edu/president/communications]. Oct. 1994.

Ziman, J. *Prometheus Bound: Science in a Dynamic Steady State.* Cambridge: Cambridge University Press, 1994.

G. DOYLE DAVES, JR., *is provost emeritus and professor of chemistry emeritus at Rensselaer Polytechnic Institute, Troy, New York.*

2

An environment for learning should be established that reflects an informed awareness of how people learn, one that prepares all students for life and work in a society dominated by science and technology and is based on the expectation that all students can learn science and mathematics.

New Truths and Old Verities

Judith A. Ramaley

America's future—its ability to create a truly just society, sustain its economic vitality, and remain secure in a world torn by hostilities—depends more than ever before on the character and quality of the education that the nation provides for its children.

To prepare all young people for lives of citizenship and social responsibility as well as success in a workplace increasingly shaped by science and technology will require some convictions. They are unlikely to understand any complex thinking unless during formal education they acquire a deep understanding of the ways of knowing of different fields and of the world. If during their education, they are never required to examine assumptions, acquired early, deeply embedded, and applied without thought to the challenges of daily life, they will not be responsive to the insights and knowledge generated by any discipline, including the sciences and mathematics. I am convinced that in a world where knowledge of science and technology is increasingly the passport to success, this limitation can mean a loss of opportunity and a barrier to any hopes for a reasonable quality of life. This need leads to the things that academic leaders should keep in mind in shaping the future of the institutions for which they are responsible. Science and mathematics must be a central part of a twenty-first-century liberal arts education. Scientists, mathematicians, engineers, and technologists have their own way of thinking about and talking about the nature of our world, man-made and natural. They have their own vocabulary, their own ways of talking about ideas and problems, their own standards of proof, and their own methodologies. All undergraduates, no matter their career aspiration, should become acquainted with these ways of knowing as approaches that are complementary to the insights offered by other

NEW DIRECTIONS FOR HIGHER EDUCATION, no. 119, Fall 2002   © Wiley Periodicals, Inc.

fields. Students should not be asked to abandon these other ways of thinking when they cross the threshold of a science or mathematics department, but rather should be challenged to see how different ways of looking at the world can help them connect what they are learning in the classroom and lab to the world they will experience beyond the campus. We must prepare all students for lives of creativity, citizenship, and social responsibility, as well as for success in a work environment increasingly shaped by science and technology.

Not only must every student become familiar with the ways of knowing and the insights of science and mathematics, but every student must master these ideas and concepts. The mantra that has emerged in K–12 education—that no child be left behind—applies with equal power to students at the undergraduate level. Our greatest vulnerability as a nation rests in the extent to which we limit the participation of all of our young people in science and mathematics and, more important, fail to expect that all students can succeed.

Learning is doing. Students who never do any science but simply read about it or are lectured about it are likely to acquire only a sense of certainty about what is known; they will gain a false impression about the scientific way of knowing: how scientific and numeric and technological understandings are attained. Those who think that science is a product rather than a process—a messy process of inquiry—can become profoundly uncomfortable when they are brought face to face with the uncertainties and arguments in the scientific arena that surface in daily life, including those that expose science and technology at the frontier. All students need to know, from firsthand experience, the strengths and limitations of scientific and mathematical reasoning.

Students learn this best by being immersed in a discovery-based learning environment. It is important to provide genuine experiences of doing science throughout the educational experience, from preschool through graduate education; link the questions addressed in this learning environment to issues that students care about; and integrate scientific exploration with other disciplines so that all students can see how understanding the different ways of knowing lead to a deeper understanding of their world and their place in this world. When science is meaningfully connected to things young people care about, it becomes a process of learning that shapes their thinking and their lives rather than a product merely to be memorized and forgotten.

This learning by doing works best in a research-rich learning environment in which faculty are as passionate about the quality of student learning as they are about their own personal research. These faculty create a research-like environment for lower-level students, recognizing that success in learning at this stage motivates students to persist and consider careers in these fields. They also see involvement in research as the key to success for those pursuing graduate studies or technical careers. There should be tangible support for research-active faculty, at all career stages, recognizing that faculty who remain active as scholars and can share that passion with their students make a difference on campus.

We are learning about how people learn but do not often use what we know. We know much about learning from the theoretical perspective, but there is a significant gap between what the education research and the cognitive science communities have learned about learning and how scientists, mathematicians, and engineers apply these theories in their scholarly work as teachers and curriculum designers. We need to find creative ways to close that gap by encouraging faculty to approach educational questions with the same habits of inquiry, rigor, and discipline that they bring to their research in the lab. It is particularly important that faculty who work with graduate students prepare them to address critical educational questions: What works? How does it work? For whom does it work? and How do we know? Campuses should establish and support learning-teaching centers through which faculty become acquainted with advances in cognitive science and learn how those understandings can inform the selection of appropriate technologies, pedagogies, and assessment practices.

Strengthening the K–16 science and mathematics community is a responsibility and an opportunity for undergraduate institutions. Attention to the preparation of the generation of K–12 science and mathematics teachers so urgently needed by our nation is one potential arena for K–16 engagement. Campuses should give careful consideration to the appropriate roles for their STEM faculty in the development of teacher preparation programs, forging connections between the disciplinary departments and the education department or school. There should also be tangible support for programs that provide opportunities for current undergraduates to work in supervised settings in K–12 classrooms and for elementary and secondary teachers to advise and learn from undergraduate faculty. For college and university faculty in STEM, the experience of working with colleagues in the education field and those from the K–12 community can open up new avenues of thinking about educational issues—how people learn—as well as develop a broader understanding of the experience of undergraduates and how to promote deeper learning of science and mathematics for all students.

A deeper understanding of the ways of knowing within different fields leads to more profound learning. Samuel Wineburg (2001) offers a helpful interpretation of the problem of public understanding of any discipline. Although he examines this question from the perspective of history, his insights apply with equal cogency to the study of science and mathematics, engineering and technology. He makes the case that "historical thinking, in its deepest forms, is neither a natural process nor something that springs automatically from psychological development" (p. 143) and argues that it is much easier to memorize facts, dates, and names of historical figures than it is "to change the basic mental structures we use to grasp the meaning of the past" (p. 146). History, in his hands, becomes an example of the challenge of any form of disciplined thinking, any process of seeking to get beyond the surface of a subject to its underlying warrants for truth.

Students are unlikely to understand the complex thinking of any discipline unless, during their formal education, they acquire a deeper understanding of the ways of knowing of that field. If they are never required to examine those deeper assumptions acquired in early years and applied without thought to the challenges of daily life, they will not be responsive to the insights and knowledge generated by any discipline, including the sciences, mathematics, and engineering.

The education of STEM majors must foster the desired qualities of a liberally educated person. In addition to learning the habits of mind and forms of expression and inquiry of science and mathematics, students majoring in a STEM field should be expected to demonstrate the qualities of a person prepared to live a life that is productive, creative, and responsible. There are many approaches to articulating the purpose of education at the undergraduate level. All involve bringing together concepts of intellectual engagement and cognitive development with the fostering of emotional maturity and social responsibility. A college graduate should be informed, open-minded, and empathetic. These qualities are not engendered solely by general education courses during the first two years of college. Science, mathematics, and engineering departments must build these expectations into their conception of the work of the major as well. It is helpful to think of an undergraduate education as a continuum of increasingly complex intellectual challenges, accompanied by increasingly complex applications with consequences of increasing significance for oneself and for others.

We know a lot about what works. As a scientist turned university administrator turned federal official, I am well aware of the problems that academic leaders face in thinking through, perhaps in reorienting, certainly in building and sustaining an environment for learning that serves their students well. What I also know is that there is a rich and stimulating set of experiences within this nation's undergraduate STEM community that can serve as a solid foundation for broader and more sustained efforts on individual campuses in all parts of this country.

As trustees, presidents, and other senior administrators make hard decisions about limited resources, they should take advantage of the lessons learned in other settings and shape the future of the programs on their campus based on those experiences. In industry, this would be called benchmarking: learning what works in other settings and adapting best practices in ways that respect local circumstances. In the not-too-distant past, such exchanging of ideas and information was difficult. From the practical perspective, it was not easy to discover colleagues doing similar work because there was no community of practice within the educational community such as that within the research communities. From the intellectual perspective, faculty seemed disposed against adapting, convinced that local exploration and invention of programs and practices that work was the only way, skeptical about ideas that were not home grown.

Yet we are now seeing collaborations, partnerships, and networks that serve the dissemination of best practices, most enabled by the sophisticated technologies now ready at hand. Academic leaders, in administrative and faculty offices alike, must take notice of the emerging National Science Digital Library, supported by the National Science Foundation. This library will be a tool by which to achieve excellence in science education at all levels, pre-K to gray.

Science is everybody's business. This goes for presidents and provosts too. The only way we can be sure that all of our nation's undergraduates will gain mastery of the ideas and ways of thinking of science and mathematics is to involve all leaders at all levels in all of our educational institutions. College and university presidents, trustees, and chief academic officers must embrace the need for a more timely and coherent conception of the undergraduate curriculum for all students. They must encourage meaningful partnerships between their institutions and K–12 communities in their region. They must connect with business and political leaders in shaping an agenda for action.

In doing this, academic leaders must come to understand why constructing undergraduate experiences for all students that incorporate a genuine involvement in science and mathematics is central to their responsibility to preserve the long-term distinctiveness and viability of their particular institution and to make a significant contribution to the good of our society.

Reference

Wineburg, S. *Historical Thinking*. Philadelphia: Temple University Press, 2001.

JUDITH A. RAMALEY is assistant director of the Education and Human Resources Directorate at the National Science Foundation, Arlington, Virginia.

PART TWO

The Curriculum and the Sequences of Learning

3

When students at any level fail to learn, we don't ask, "What are we doing wrong?" or "Should we attempt a different pedagogical approach or a different motivational strategy?" We simply deduce that they are not smart enough.

Changing Assumptions About Who Can Learn

George Campbell, Jr.

Higher education, particularly in the sciences, is facing a number of stimulating and challenging questions as the various disciplines unfold. A fundamental shift is taking place, for example, between the physical and biological sciences. Complex physical systems, such as communications networks, increasingly resemble complex adaptive biological systems. The overall scientific underpinning of technology is shifting from the physical sciences to the life sciences, to biological processes at the molecular level, to genomics, to bioinformatics, to evolutionary algorithms, and DNA computing. That is, technology is increasingly being driven by advances in our understanding of the life sciences rather than the physical sciences.

In the midst of these enormous, dramatic, and rapid changes, higher education faces a number of critical questions:

- How should our curriculum evolve in the context of the changing environment?
- What new pedagogical paradigms must emerge as we move more deeply into the information age?
- What are the most effective ways of exploiting technology to strengthen the learning environment in each of our academic disciplines without sacrificing intellectual rigor and without stifling creativity, a genuine risk with neatly packaged computer programs and simulations?

This chapter is excerpted from a plenary address given at the Project Kaleidoscope 2001 Summer Institute.

NEW DIRECTIONS FOR HIGHER EDUCATION, no. 119, Fall 2002 © Wiley Periodicals, Inc.

- What is the correct balance among research, teaching, and pedagogical efforts?

One crucial issue is our inadequate success in developing the full potential of students in the sciences from all economic and ethnic backgrounds. Another important question, then, is:

- What are the root causes of our failure as a nation to develop a more diverse cadre of students and to bring them into the natural sciences, mathematics, and engineering professions?

The ascendance of the United States to world power status in the nineteenth century was facilitated by the introduction of public education and the concept of universal access to education. Looking to the future, I believe that our success as both a nation and a global society will be similarly facilitated by universal access to high-quality higher education with a healthy dose of science and mathematics. Throughout human history, science and engineering, and their predecessor professions, have been the principal driving forces behind economic development, wealth creation, and upward mobility. But effective universal higher education is also critical to cultural evolution; the progress of human civilization; and improved human interaction and understanding across cultural, ethnic, and national boundaries, which, in the post–cold war era, has become perhaps the central issue of our time.

Access to higher education is rooted in the earlier stages of education, the feeder system. Those of us in higher education have an important role to play in that arena as well. Since the public schools in America were introduced almost a century and a half ago, the nation has delivered widely varying quality in education. From the beginning, only a small subset of the population has received what can be called a superb education. In the industrial age, that was quite adequate. What was needed to make the industrial economy work was a universally literate population but only a handful of highly educated individuals.

Today, we still provide a high-quality education to only a handful of students. On average, students who live in suburban communities have access to higher-quality schools than those who live in rural or inner-city communities, as do wealthy students compared to poor students and white students compared to black students. But today 80 percent of the workforce is engaged in creating, processing, or disseminating information, and it is no longer adequate to provide a high-quality education to a small percentage of students. The information age economy demands a high-level education for the masses. It demands a considerably higher proportion of college graduates than we have produced in the past.

Within the complex of precollege education problems in the United States today, a persistent, pervasive weakness is in mathematics and science.

The statistics are appalling. Only 16 percent of American students take the full complement of high school mathematics and science courses through calculus and physics. Only 7 percent of African American, Latino, and Native American students take calculus and physics. Approximately half do not take math beyond algebra II (National Science Board, 2002). By contrast, in many other nations around the world, calculus and physics are required courses for all students in high school.

We must ask why these trends persist in a nation that for decades has been the world's leading innovator in science and technology and what the response of academic leaders should be in considering those trends.

A personal story is illuminating on this issue. I joined Bell Labs fresh out of graduate school in the 1970s, when it was arguably the world's premiere research institution. Bell Labs also had a history of leadership in the corporate sector, opening its doors to black scientists as early as the 1940s. At one point while I was there, we estimated that Bell Labs employed about 15 percent of all active black physicists in the country, and there were some years when half of the black Ph.D. recipients in chemistry and physics were Bell Labs corporate research fellows.

This was the aftermath of the civil rights movement, and I would suggest that we had a social responsibility to find highly capable scientists in nontraditional places. We had an obligation, for example, to look beyond the top-ranked research universities because scientists with enormous talent emerging from poor communities or from minority communities were less likely to be found in those places. This is what I thought affirmative action was all about: not lowering standards and not offering preferential treatment, but making sure that we did not miss opportunities to identify exceptional individuals because of artificial barriers that veiled their potential or their abilities. The response was typically, "This is Bell Labs. We don't really have to do that. Anyone smart enough to be here is bound to come to our attention."

I cite this anecdote because I think those words embody an elitist perspective common among scientists. They embrace a whole set of assumptions that lie at the root of our problem in delivering science education. And these assumptions have enormous consequences in the context of our responsibility to deliver educational programs that compel all students to achieve their highest potential.

The most fundamental assumption, and one that is prevalent, is the idea that "smart" is a well-defined, quantitative, measurable attribute, distinct from knowledge in some particular area of human thought. There is nothing wrong with the idea that intelligence exists. What is egregious is the belief that intelligence is an innate, genetic attribute, an immutable quality: one either has it at birth or does not, and nothing can be done to change it. Cognitive scientists are far from unanimous on this subject.

Although there is a cadre of highly respected cognitive scientists who believe that the range of human intellectual potential is quite narrow and that human beings have the ability to increase intelligence, that is, to become "smart," the innate, immutable intelligence model is deeply ingrained in our educational system from preschool through graduate school. Consequently, our educational institutions are organized not to identify, develop, and nurture the intelligence and intellectual potential of all students, but rather to measure intelligence, to sort students based on the outcomes of those measurements, and to deliver education differentially depending on how and where students fit into the ill-defined categories. Whether they are formally tracked or not, this deeply ingrained concept of intelligence yields a very effective informal tracking process that I believe results in the dismal numbers of minorities active in scientific and technological fields in this country today. Ability grouping is used, consciously or subconsciously, as a mechanism to perpetuate racial and economic class segregation in higher education too.

We agree that students of the same age can be at different places on the intellectual development curve, but research overwhelmingly shows that students at all academic levels benefit from heterogeneous groupings. More advanced students deepen their understanding through discourse with those less advanced, who benefit from the skills and knowledge of their more advanced colleagues. More important, research also shows the value of diversity of perspectives and ways of thinking as groups work together on projects or assignments in academic, corporate, and business settings.

Yet even as we know all this, minority students in educational environments are disproportionally placed in low-ability groups from which there is very little opportunity to escape, because they are given watered-down curricula, poorly trained teachers, and few resources. Assumptions about students' abilities are often based on superficial characteristics, styles of dress or cultural attributes, or patterns of behavior that are unrelated to academic skills or potential. The implications for local and national efforts to diversify the scientific and engineering communities are chilling. That mathematics and science are regarded as difficult subjects, appropriate only for students regarded as having high ability, to a large extent accounts for the low numbers of students taking advanced mathematics and science courses.

A few years ago, I was on a national commission looking at the reform of education in mathematics. When it became clear from the work of California educator Jaime Escalante and others that the fundamental principles of calculus were not too difficult for all students to learn after all, the next questions by commission members were, "But where do we draw the line? Is it at differential equations? Can students of average intelligence be expected to master linear algebra?" There was a complete unwillingness to give up the assumption that at some fairly low level, mathematics is beyond the reach of all but a few select students. Psychologists Harold Stevenson and James Stigler (1992) made a comparative study of the American system of education with that of East Asian countries. Their conclusion was that the reason students in other countries significantly outperformed those in the United States is precisely that educators in those countries assume that all students can learn at a high level.

The bottom line is that no amount of spending, no amount of curriculum reform, no amount of national testing or educational technology will solve our educational problems as long as teachers, professors, and other academic leaders believe that the vast majority of students are not capable of learning mathematics and science. This perspective is a major inhibiting factor in local and national efforts to diversify the scientific and engineering workforce.

The statistics reveal that we have a long way to go (Hill, 2000). In 1997, fewer than 1 percent of the Ph.D.s awarded to computer scientists (4 out of 905) went to African Americans. Seventeen went to graduate students who were Mexican Americans or Puerto Ricans. In mathematics, the Ph.D. productivity for minorities is equally bleak. In that same year, there were 7 African Americans and eighteen Hispanics out of 1,125 doctoral degrees awarded. In my field, physics, over the past twenty-five years in the pool of roughly 1,000 Ph.D.s a year, typically 5 to 10 were African American. In the history of this country, only about twenty-five African American women have received a Ph.D. in physics. These facts, given the global competition for scientific talent, does not bode well for the future of science in the United States, particularly at a time when more than 50 percent of those under eighteen years old in the United States are members of groups underrepresented in the study and practice of science and engineering (National Science and Technology Council, 2000).

The university, as a central repository of intellectual capital and those leading this country's colleges and universities, has a considerable responsibility to bring those precious resources to bear on critical social issues. The lack of diversity in the scientific and engineering communities is one of those critical issues that involves us all directly.

If we want to address the access problem in a comprehensive way, we have to reach well beyond our ivory towers in the way that I was urging Bell Labs to cast a wider net decades ago. Academic leaders must make the commitment to invest the resources to make this happen, and some fundamental assumptions have to change. We must all realize that vast numbers of students in the United States with highly developed intellectual and analytical skills are languishing in thoroughly unstimulating classrooms in which the level of instruction is beneath the minimum level of cognitive potential of the students. Once this is realized, programs and curricula can be better shaped to serve all students.

References

Hill, S. *Science and Engineering Degrees, by Race/Ethnicity: 1989–1997*. Arlington, Va.: National Science Foundation, Division of Science Resources Studies, 2000.

National Science Board. *Science and Engineering Indicators—2002*. Arlington, Va.: National Science Foundation, 2002.

National Science and Technology Council. *Ensuring a Strong U.S. Scientific, Technical, and Engineering Workforce in the Twenty-First Century/* Washington, D.C.: Executive Office of the President, 2000. [http://clinton4.nara.gov/pdf/workforcept.pdf].

Stevenson, H., and Stigler, J. *The Learning Gap.* New York: Summit Books, 1992.

GEORGE CAMPBELL, JR., is president of the Cooper Union for the Advancement of Science and Art, New York, New York.

4

Setting goals for student learning in fields of science, technology, and mathematics must receive institutionwide attention, setting expectations for what graduates should know and developing departmental and programmatic course offerings that ensure those expectations will be met.

Science for All Americans

George D. Nelson

A very distinguished scientist told me one day that he agreed that 10 percent of the students learn the material in any class on their own. In the same conversation, he also commented on how discouraged he was about students coming into his classes. And then he said, "Well, I only teach to the top 10 percent anyway. If the rest of them don't get it, what difference does it make?" I responded, "Let's see, now, we know that 10 percent aren't going to learn no matter what you do, and you teach only to the top 10 percent. Hmmm."

I propose a ten-year project for leaders in higher education, working with leaders from the K–12 community. The goal would be that all students who graduate from postsecondary institutions would be literate in science and mathematics and technology at the level for high school graduates outlined in *Science for All Americans* (1990), the major publication of Project 2061, founded by the American Association for the Advancement of Science in 1985 to help all Americans become literate in science, mathematics, and technology. Such a goal would be the same as we have set for the K–12 community. To accomplish this, we will have to change the mind-set that only the top 10 percent can or should have access to the best learning in these fields. We have to teach to the top 90 percent, not the top 10 percent. These are the future parents, teachers, and citizens, and we must expect them all to learn at the literacy level. If we can achieve this, graduating from our universities and colleges teachers, parents, and citizens who are literate in mathematics, science, and technology, perhaps ten years from now we will see a significant impact in the schools and in our public life.

This chapter is excerpted from a plenary address made at the 2000 Project Kaleidoscope Summer Institute, Keystone, Colorado, July 19, 2000.

The good news is that attention to the 90 percent is being done in many places. There are huge resources of expertise and experience in the field, and no one needs to reinvent the wheel. There is not enough time, or enough money, to reinvent the wheel. This work of teaching to the 90 percent toward a ten-year goal of literacy should be approached, at the individual level, as you would approach a research project. Anyone who is starting a new effort or moving into a new direction in research explores in the library, on the Web, and at conferences to find out what others are doing, what directions their research is taking them, who the people are to connect to, learn from, and collaborate with. The intent is to study what others have done and build on their work. In this effort, I urge taking advantage of those in the K–12 community who are getting things done.

The first step in a ten-year project is to define the goals. So we must ask, "What is important for students to learn?" To answer that question, take a close look at materials from Project 2061: *Science for All Americans* (American Association for the Advancement of Science, 1990) or the Benchmarks for Science Literacy (American Association for the Advancement of Science, 1995). Or study carefully the National Science Education Standards (National Research Council, 1996) and the mathematics standards from the National Council of Teachers of Mathematics (2000). These are among the several essential resources outlining the content and skills students need to know. That does not mean faculty cannot talk about black holes or other topics not in the standards as a vehicle to get students to learn. These documents make it clear, however, that the learning goal for all students is an understanding of science—an understanding of how science works and how numbers work, with an understanding of the fundamental ways of thinking that drive these fields.

Worrying about what we want students to learn is critical, and I believe that this is something those who wish to be leaders in higher education need to give more attention to. Much time has been spent on the how of student learning, exploring and discovering that students learn differently if they work in groups, or that if faculty design interactive lectures, students become engaged in building their own ideas. I hope we can figure out how to combine thinking about changing how we teach with thinking about changing what we teach.

Science for All Americans is about what all people should know about math, science, and technology ten years after graduating from university or college. I include those planning to be scientists and engineers, or physicists who might need to know something about biology, or biologists who might need to know something about engineering. Our goal must be that all students leave our high schools and undergraduate campuses with the habits of mind that make them scientifically and quantitatively literate.

The first step is for college and university faculty to come to greater clarity and precision about how and what they teach and how and what students learn.

The second step is using the research on learning in teaching. The significant research now being done on how people learn is making important discoveries. One is that we need to address people from where they are. Students do not come into classrooms as blank slates. They come with preconceptions and with misconceptions. Unless the instructor understands the need to elicit their ideas from them and make them confront their own thinking as they confront the phenomena of the physical world, students will not change their ways of thinking. Their misconceptions are incredibly resilient. Research makes it clear that people only learn by having to recognize their own thinking in the context of confronting other ways of thinking.

We are also learning that people do not learn unless they are made to reflect on their own learning, on their own thinking, and this needs to be incorporated in the classrooms and labs. None of this will make the lives of instructors any easier, but recognizing that helping students learn requires knowing subject matter and knowing about teaching and learning. And that is precisely the responsibility of professors.

This means, at its most fundamental, that professors must have real expectations for students, that all students should be expected to learn. Research on how people learn, and the experience of many academics, makes it clear that high expectations within the learning environment build confidence and motivate students to succeed. And the expectations should be that students are learning real science, have access to robust programs in mathematics, and come to understand the nature of scientific and quantitative thinking in ways that they understand how this has an impact on individuals and on society.

I once proposed a "Poetry for Physicists" course to the English department at the university at which I was teaching; that department had complained to the physics department about the rigor of the university's "Physics for Poets." I proposed to start with Hallmark cards and work my way through the quarter up to Dr. Seuss; the proposal was not accepted. But I made my point that the idea is not to water down the poetry that students learn or the physics that they learn, but to prune it, carefully selecting some key ideas, and really diving in and learning them deeply, so the students understand something about physics or biology or poetry in their bones. Most students have never really learned anything at that level, and it turns out that digging deeply into a field is incredibly exciting. It is also my experience that for students, the sheer joy of learning something really well is an incredible motivator.

This is a radical proposal: that by 2011, all students graduating from American colleges and universities will be literate at the level of *Science for All Americans*. It will mean that much will have to change in both what and how teaching and learning take place on college campuses. It will also require moving away from the silos of a geology sequence or a physics or biology sequence to an environment for learning designed so that students come to understand the connections among the disciplines: how mathematical modeling connects with biology or the impact of technology on science, for example.

Although the end of this project is far away, the urgency is such that we had better get started now. This will take a full court press at the institutional level. Faculty who are eager to rethink the what and how of their teaching should identify colleagues who are willing to be so engaged. Not everyone will be involved at first, of course. The point is to begin discussions about goals for student learning and expectations for student learning now, and then begin working together to broaden and sustain these discussions within the local community and move to action. The experience of productive reforms suggests that administrators are supportive when faculty have set ambitious goals.

I hope that the tools and the things that we are doing in Project 2061—developing age-appropriate benchmarks or standards for student learning, curriculum materials analysis and evaluation, workshops for faculty and professional development, CD-ROMs, and on-line aids for educators and administrators—will continue to help provide resources for professors in their work and that as time goes on, Project 2061, Project Kaleidoscope, and the higher education community in general can become more and more intertwined and involved with each other in working toward our common goal.

References

American Association for the Advancement of Science, Project 2061. *Science for All Americans, Project 2061.* New York: Oxford University Press, 1990.

American Association for the Advancement of Science, Project 2061. *Benchmarks for Science Literacy.* Washington, D.C.: American Association for the Advancement of Science, 1995.

National Council of Teachers of Mathematics. *Principles and Standards for School Mathematics.* Reston, Va.: National Council of Teachers of Mathematics, 2000.

National Research Council. *National Science Education Standards.* Washington, D.C.: National Academy Press, 1996.

GEORGE D. NELSON *is director of science, mathematics, and technology education at Western Washington University, Bellingham.*

5

A major research university makes a commitment to give students not majoring in science or engineering a solid foundation in scientific and quantitative thinking through an integrated large-scale, multidisciplinary three-course sequence.

A Multidisciplinary Core Curriculum

Trace Jordan

One of the challenges of higher education is to help all students become literate citizens, well equipped to deal with the many important personal and societal decisions that now require a firm foundation in mathematical, quantitative, and scientific reasoning. Discussions on whether statistical sampling should be used in the national census, debates on the appropriate level of federal funding for stem cell research, and evaluation of the appropriate response to the problem of global warming are examples of decisions that citizens are now being called on to make. In addition, today's students should appreciate science as a central component of human inquiry about the natural world. The scientific community continues to generate exciting discoveries, ranging from the large-scale structure of the universe to the microscopic-scale existence of organisms in extreme environments.

Unfortunately, students who do not major in a scientific discipline often receive a level of science education that is inadequate for comprehending contemporary scientific and technological achievements. The lack of knowledge on the part of many college graduates is identified as a critical problem by many, including a recent report, commissioned by the National Research Council (1999), that examined the current state of science, mathematics, engineering, and technology education: "The understanding of SME&T by most Americans, which reflects the level of SME&T education that most Americans have had, is inadequate for full participation in this increasingly technological world. Our nation is becoming divided into a technologically knowledgeable elite and a disadvantaged majority" (p. 1).

New York University (NYU) has made a strong commitment to general mathematics and science education for its undergraduate students. In 1995, the College of Arts and Science established a new core curriculum, the Morse

Academic Plan (MAP) after Samuel F. B. Morse, an artist, inventor of the telegraph, and an early NYU faculty member. In addition to course sequences in the humanities and social sciences, expository writing, and foreign language, the MAP curriculum includes a three-course sequence, Foundations of Scientific Inquiry (FSI), specifically designed for nonmajors who do not wish to take majors-level courses. Within each unit—"Quantitative Reasoning," "Natural Science I," and "Natural Science II"—several different courses are offered, thereby allowing students to choose the one that best matches their interests.

The first unit in the sequence, "Quantitative Reasoning" (QR), provides students with a foundation in mathematics, emphasizing topics such as graphical representation, algebraic formulation, and the application of mathematical reasoning to real-world problems. An important component of the QR courses is the weekly workshop where students collaborate on solving mathematical problems under the guidance of a trained graduate student. Course offerings in QR include "Mathematical Patterns in Nature," which investigates the application of mathematics in the physics sciences, and "Mathematical Patterns in Society," which explores mathematical principles in the context of the social sciences. Another course, "Mathematics and the Computer," blends the study of logic and Boolean algebra with the practical application of these mathematical ideas in digital electronics. Its workshop projects train students to proceed from a symbolic representation of logical operations to building a circuit using logic gates to perform a particular computational function.

The following units, "Natural Science I" and "Natural Science II," focus on physical sciences and life sciences, respectively. Some versions use contemporary scientific topics as a framework for teaching students both core scientific principles and the process of scientific investigation. Others employ a historical approach to demonstrate the development of scientific ideas.

All of the natural science courses have a laboratory component, where students perform experiments and generate scientific conclusions based on their own data. Most of the laboratory projects have been developed in-house, with an emphasis on experiments that connect closely to the lecture topics. The inclusion of a laboratory component in the FSI program reflects the belief by the NYU faculty and administration that students can best understand the process of scientific investigation by actively participating in it themselves. The laboratories are taught by graduate students from the science departments, who work under the close supervision of the faculty instructor and MAP staff. Most laboratory sessions are located in the Science Education Center in the college's main building, which contains dedicated facilities built in 1996 for the new core curriculum.

The offerings in the unit "Natural Science I" include "Einstein's Universe," where students study the life and science of Albert Einstein, including his contributions to relativity and the quantum nature of light.

The course concludes by exploring how Einstein's ideas are being challenged and extended by modern cosmologists, including ideas such as inflation and the experimental study of black holes. Another course in the physical sciences is "Energy and the Environment," which examines the scientific foundations and policy decisions for current environmental issues such as global warming, water pollution, and renewable sources of energy. Within the "Natural Science II" rubric, the "Brain and Behavior" course explores our current understanding of the brain and the biological basis of behavior, whereas the "Human Origins" course integrates the scientific study of primate behavior, genetic variation, and paleontology in a multidisciplinary investigation of human evolution.

The FSI program began in the College of Arts and Science and has since expanded to include undergraduates from the Stern School of Business, the Steinhardt School of Education, and the School of Continuing and Professional Studies. Enrollment in all three FSI courses now exceeds fifteen hundred students each semester, so the program is making a widespread impact in mathematics and science education for nonmajors. All courses are taught by regular faculty in the Faculty of Arts and Science. Academic oversight and educational leadership for the program is provided by a faculty steering committee, whose membership includes the dean of the college, the dean for science, and the chairs of the mathematics and science departments. The program is administered by the MAP director, an assistant director and a coordinator for FSI, and the assistant director for MAP administration. The director, the faculty committee, and the MAP staff report to the dean of the College of Arts and Science. Laboratory experiments for students are provided by a dedicated laboratory facility with four full-time staff members, who also assist the faculty and MAP staff with laboratory design.

The Foundations of Scientific Inquiry program constitutes a large-scale, multidisciplinary core curriculum that is directly addressing the educational challenge of mathematical and scientific literacy for undergraduate students. We will continue to refine and improve the program, with a special emphasis on assessing students' gains in understanding science and its relevance to modern society.

Reference

National Research Council, Committee on Undergraduate Science Education. *Transforming Undergraduate Education in Science, Mathematics, Engineering, and Technology*. Washington, D.C.: National Academy Press, 1999.

TRACE JORDAN *is assistant director for the Morse Academic Plan at New York University, New York, New York.*

By giving concerted attention to each of the junctures at which students were being lost to the study of science and mathematics, a community of K–16 educators realizes greater success and persistence for its students.

Building Natural Science Communities

Thomas E. Brady

The University of Texas at El Paso (UTEP) has an enrollment of 15,500 students, of whom 69 percent are Hispanic and over 71 percent are from groups recognized as underrepresented in the study and practice of science and engineering. This includes the more than 50 percent of students who are women. Although located in a vibrant community, one enriched by its ethnic diversity, the challenge for UTEP has been to make education accessible to all students within its service area. This is a geographically isolated region of the country, with limited educational and economic opportunities for most people, and UTEP has faced special challenges in ensuring the access to quality education expected by the larger society and by local community members.

The challenges are many, beginning with the reality that vast numbers of potential students have been effectively shut out of the university because of the dismal preparation they received in the region's elementary and secondary schools. But UTEP's story is little different from that of similar institutions. In Texas, less than 60 percent of Hispanic eighteen year olds are high school graduates, and within the group of those who have persevered through graduation, over 75 percent did not take the Scholastic Aptitude Test. Since UTEP draws about 85 percent of its students from the resident county and provides more than half of the teachers for county schools, this leaky pipeline of students is disconcerting.

That El Paso is, in essence, a closed-loop educational system from K–16 suggested possible solutions to the problem; any attempt to improve or reform one segment of this loop meant that the entire loop needed to be involved. What happened was that a remarkable collaboration of school superintendents and K–12 teachers, faculty and staff from the community college and UTEP, and business and civic leaders came together around the El Paso Collaborative for Academic Excellence.

Those of us in the collaborative set two goals for ourselves: to ensure academic success of all students in area schools K–16 and to ensure that all students graduate from area high schools well prepared to enter into and proceed well through studies at a four-year college or university by giving them a stronger grounding in mathematics, which was seen as the area of study that marked students for subsequent success. We developed a three-pronged approach:

- Develop and implement a standards-based curriculum of the highest quality in mathematics in the region's K–12 schools, an effort involving leaders from the schools and the higher education communities.
- Strengthen and enhance programs at UTEP that prepare teachers for service in the greater El Paso community.
- Engage leaders and parents, teachers, and faculty from all parts of the El Paso community.

After eight years, our success is clear: nearly 100 percent of El Paso high school students are enrolling in "Algebra I" (from 60 percent), and students from the community are ranking significantly higher than in the past on the Texas Assessment of Academic Skills exams. None of this could have been accomplished if only a single partner had set out to achieve the goal; it took much planning, rethinking, and reshaping academic programs, building new kinds of bridges between the various stakeholders, and much hard work. From UTEP's perspective, this had to be done if the institution was to reach the goal set of increasing the number of Hispanics entering careers in science, mathematics, and engineering.

Working at the K–12 level was not the entire solution. Increasing the numbers of students prepared for and entering the university was not enough if they failed early on and were not motivated to persist. We knew that we had a responsibility to students we admitted to ensure that they succeeded. This effort too involved many people in different spheres of responsibility across several divisions of the campus. Making use of the university's unique location and opportunity as a living laboratory for on-site research in social, human, economic, environmental, and health-related issues, we developed educational and research programs to meet the challenge of serving the diverse multicultural population that is our constituency.

Two activities are of special note. First, recognizing that it was during their first year that students become frustrated, convinced that they could not learn science and mathematics, we designed a comprehensive program targeting first-year students in science, mathematics, and engineering (first-time freshmen and new transfers): Circles of Learning for Entering Students (CirCLES). This provides a mechanism to cluster courses of appropriate levels in mathematics and English for students indicating an interest in majoring in these fields. They also sign up for a university seminar that involves academic peer support groups. To stay in the group, students must (1) participate in summer orientation and advising programs, (2) enroll full time in the fall semester, (3) be a first-time freshman at the university (with no more than twenty-nine transfer hours), and (4) be a declared science, engineering, or mathematics (SEM) major.

Since the 1997 pilot group, over a thousand entering SEM students have participated in CirCLES. We track these students with great care, noting retention, success, and graduation rates. The number of hours attempted and completed is an important indicator of student commitment and potential for continued success. CirCLES students, on average, rank high on this indicator.

The second strategy to improve the persistence of declared majors is to involve them deeply in laboratory research programs. Just as with the K–16 collaborative and CirCLES, which were funded by the National Science Foundation, it took external grants to achieve a critical mass of faculty and students engaged as colleagues in research. Support from the National Institutes of Health was critical here. Research on these engaged students documents that being active in a research community and working closely on a regular basis with a mentor has a positive impact on their professional and personal goals. They are more positive and vocal about pursuing careers in these fields, clearer about what it takes to be a successful student and practitioner in SEM fields, and more confident about their capacity to succeed in graduate school. As with the CirCLES program, numbers again tell the story of success. In the fall of 2000, over 84 percent of the involved students indicated an interest in graduate school.

The shortage of minority students interested in becoming practicing scientists or engineers is a national disgrace. If we do not capture the attention of all students and stretch their imagination that they have a future in these fields, there will be a loss of talent in the service of this country that we can ill afford. The efforts at UTEP and on many other campuses suggest that significant progress can be made when students are expected to succeed and a structure is put in place to see that they do. The concept of the CirCLES program has been adapted and adopted by the UTEP for all entering students, not just declared SEM majors.

THOMAS E. BRADY is dean of science at University of Texas at El Paso.

7

If academic leaders are serious about enhancing student learning, then what we are learning about how people learn from research in cognitive science must guide the redesign of higher education.

Cognitive Science and the Work of Reform

Diane F. Halpern

What we know about how people think, how they learn, and how they remember should be central to educational reform efforts, especially in fields like mathematics, science, engineering, and technology that have seen a literal explosion of knowledge. The United States has a serious shortage of scientists and others with the skills for productive careers in a technological world. Most distressing of all is a low level of understanding of scientific and numeric principles and methods within the general public. By using what is known about human cognition, we can enhance how much and how well students learn. Powerful models of human learning exist that can be used as a guide for the redesign of education at the undergraduate level, and higher education needs to be redesigned. Virtually every variable in the higher education equation is changing at a rapidly accelerating rate. Change is hard, and universities and colleges do not take kindly to it.

My academic area is cognitive psychology, an empirical branch of psychology that deals with how people think, how they learn, and how they remember. Cognitive psychologists study how people acquire, use, organize, and retrieve information. They study topics such as memory, decision making, problem identification and solving, critical thinking, and reasoning. A successful pedagogical philosophy that will serve as a basis for learning must incorporate understandings about the way in which learners acquire and organize information. This philosophy must address how students represent knowledge internally, the way they store it (that is, keep it in their minds), the way these representations change, and the way they resist change over time.

Despite all the recent gains made in understanding what happens when people learn, the truth is that most professors have gained relatively little from cognitive psychology. Even cognitive psychologists apply very little about what they know about their discipline in their own teaching. There is a tremendous gap between empirically validated theories and pedagogical practice. This hit me most directly when sitting through one of those deadly dull, three-hour graduate school lectures, and I realized the topic was "The Shortness of the Human Attention Span." It was at that moment I realized the reality of the gap between what we know and what we do about learning.

Virtually all college-level courses in math, science, and engineering, particularly at the introductory level, involve a lecture portion. This means a class with a lone professor who is talking and writing on the board and some students who are taking notes. This is a satisfactory arrangement for learning if the desired outcome is to have students recognize the correct answer on a multiple-choice test. In the language of cognitive psychology, this is a recognition test; we want students to recognize, that is, generate, the correct answer, which is the one closest to what they learned in class. And we know it is possible for students to get a high score on recognition tests yet not be able to recognize a concept in a slightly altered context; neither will they be able to apply that concept in another course later in their academic career.

One problem this causes is when courses are sequential and students are expected to carry forward knowledge from one class to another. "What did the professor before me teach them? Why don't they know it?" a professor asks. His colleague replies, "Well, here's my exam. They all got the right answers." That lectures alone are too often a useless expenditure of force has been known for generations, and in cultures beyond this country, before recent advances in cognitive science.

Lectures are of benefit when there is a lot of information to get across in a short period of time and the students are already thinking, have a good background in the subject, and are committed to learning. But the most important variable in why and what and how much something gets learned is not what professors do; it is what students do. This means attention to what we ask them to do with the materials we want them to know. The old expression in psychology, "The head remembers what it does," is another way to validate the discovery-based research learning environments that are emerging on campuses across the country.

What does not work, from the perspective of cognitive science, is laboratory experiments that are canned, particularly at the introductory level. These require very little original thought by the learners; they experience very few surprises in the process of learning except perhaps when something does not work. If the goal is to excite students about science and mathematics, it does no good to use approaches to learning that bear little resemblance to those cognitive processes used in these fields. There is another tremendous gap here: between how science is taught and how it is practiced. The more creative aspects of the scientific community—generating a real question, exploring those multiple decision points made in research—are completely invisible to students, especially at the introductory level. And it is at this level that the vast majority of college students complete their formal education in science and mathematics. I do not know how many students have been turned off by canned or cookbook labs who might have had some creativity or interest sparked if they had had more of that kind of involvement in exploring: What is the right question? How might we make this decision?

As another example, asking learners to recall certain information on a recognition test leaves a selective forgetting of related information that they are not asked to recall. We know from cognitive psychology that the very act of remembering strengthens some memory traces at the same time as it weakens memory for information one is not asked to recall. Very few college faculty know this and therefore do not design what they ask their students to do (in exams or other learning activities) in a way that fits into a larger plan for what they want students to retain.

The same is true for frequent testing. When students are tested frequently, at the end of every chapter or the end of every week, they score high on those quizzes. This student success creates the impression for the faculty member that frequent testing is a good thing because students are getting high scores. In fact, such frequent testings involve very short retention intervals and lead to overconfidence because both learners and professors believe that long-term retention will be better than it really will be. This is but one example where the short-term benefits of an educational practice like frequent testing have long-term detriments. Because we do not look at retention in the long term, we do not understand what happens when the semester is over and the context for learning is changed.

Cognitive psychology and learning theory have much to offer in guiding how we design and re-form higher education. Enhancing student learning is the most important task of college professors. Higher education faculty and administrators are entrusted with the job of designing and delivering first-rate learning opportunities. They can do a better job of really educating our country's most precious commodity: smart, educated adults who can cope with and chart the direction of change.

The rate at which knowledge is growing is exponential. And the most valued asset of any society is a knowledgeable and thinking citizenry. Human capital is our wisest investment. It will take vision and persistence to prepare students to learn efficiently and think critically, so the United States can remain competitive and cooperative.

DIANE F. HALPERN *is director of the Berger Institute for Work, Family and Children at Claremont McKenna College, Claremont, California.*

8

Assessment can result in a better match between educational goals and student involvement in achieving them.

Effective Assessment and Institutional Change

Christine Brooks Cote, Marianne Jordan

At Bowdoin College, we have seen evidence that assessment is an important component of educational planning and can lead to institutional change. We regard assessment as the process of systematically gathering information to use in making decisions about educational programs. We know that discussions related to assessment can cause people to think differently about their ideas, influence faculty to make adjustments to programs as they are being implemented, and lead top-level decision makers to implement changes in educational activities, programs, and curricula that they would have been unable to imagine without the information that comes from assessment. Assessment is feedback, and feedback helps ground us in our decision making, moving us forward.

Faculty are often reluctant to carry out an assessment plan, even if they have some sense of its importance. They may believe that assessment is always related to accreditation, that is, something undertaken by administrators to satisfy the needs of the regional accrediting agency. We believe that assessment is an essential and integral part of every institution that enthusiastically and consistently endeavors to strive for excellence. We have tried to overcome this reluctance to assess by injecting assessment into one way that faculty connect with educational innovation: securing external support for new and expanding curriculum and research programs and projects.

This effort to weave assessment into the fabric of Bowdoin is a partnership between us: One of us is the director of corporate and foundation relations and the other the director of institutional research. Having collaborated informally on a number of grants, we spoke with senior administrators and established a more public relationship that shows the useful

NEW DIRECTIONS FOR HIGHER EDUCATION, no. 119, Fall 2002 © Wiley Periodicals, Inc.

45

connection between assessment and program development. Tied tightly to the design of new programs from the very beginning, assessment will be a positive tool for effecting long-lasting and vital change on campus. It took us several conversations to arrive at a consensus that setting up institutional criteria for assessment in the process of developing new proposals would ultimately benefit the college as well as the faculty member seeking funding for research or a curriculum innovation.

We see three ways in which assessment connects to programs:

• *Program planning.* Because most people think of assessment as something that happens when the program is finished, it is surprising for many faculty to realize the ways in which assessment can help at the very beginning, when an idea—a new approach to teaching, a curricular modification, or a faculty development program—is being explored and clarified. Because designing a plan for assessment necessitates clarifying the idea and goals of any project as well as thinking about the hoped-for outcomes of the project, assessment becomes a helpful part of the process of thinking through the idea. The clarity that has come to planning by having someone familiar with the principles and techniques of assessment cannot be overestimated.

• *Program implementation.* Evaluators use the term *formative evaluation* to talk about the techniques used to gather feedback while the program is in place, when project directors can use feedback in making adjustments and improving the program. This is not necessarily a new notion to faculty; many are familiar with making adjustments in a course when things are not going particularly well. The idea is the same: gather meaningful data, use them to understand what is happening, and adjust the program accordingly.

• *Program summation.* This is the final exam, the summative evaluation, and faculty understand this well. This is the point at which project or program implementers use assessment techniques to determine whether they have met their goals and objectives. But there is more. Leery of the possibility of reductionism coming from assessment, faculty have been excited by the way in which we have used assessment to determine the broad impact of the program, as well as the unanticipated outcomes. This is often the most exciting part of the assessment. Project directors analyze the data, review the findings, and absorb interview transcripts. The ensuing discussion leads people to see that the program had a greater, more varied impact than anyone predicted. Because the faculty or project directors implemented the program with the critical mind-set that accompanies assessment, change occurred, and often it was unanticipated change. Then the cycle begins again. The faculty see the next step emerging from the findings of the assessment, and a new idea is born. Now familiar with the process of assessment, faculty members see its applications to course design, student evaluation, curriculum development, and more. As a result, the institution becomes more and more attuned to change.

What we have arrived at is a team that works with faculty on all institutional grants. This has brought coherence to our assessment practices overall and helps avoid the faculty's frustration of writing an assessment component into their proposals. The advice of this team is offered through the dean's office, thus giving the team's work an institutional stamp of approval. The team leaders (grants officer and institutional research director) train faculty who are preparing to write proposals on the nuts and bolts of an assessment plan from the perspective of the specific aims of their proposed project; attention is also given to how the project will work and the institutional goals into which that project must fit. They then move to the sidelines, where they can serve as coaches, reviewing and editing proposal drafts as they emerge from the faculty.

As faculty and other administrators have become more familiar and comfortable with evaluation, they have begun using it as a lens for reexamining their courses and assessing other parts of the curriculum. Here is one example of how the process worked to benefit all concerned: the faculty member with a new idea, the students in his classroom and lab, and the broader Bowdoin culture and community.

A biology faculty member had been working out an idea for teaching introductory biology differently. The enrollments in introductory biology courses at Bowdoin are large (for a liberal arts college): about a hundred each semester, totaling two hundred students per year, or nearly half of the first-year class. Due to the size of the classes, students do not get much one-on-one time with the professor, a hallmark of strong undergraduate science programs.

The professor, a developmental biologist with a talent for developing creative, animated software, approached the head of Bowdoin's Educational Technology Center (ETC) with an idea for personalizing the introductory biology experience. The head of the ETC was supportive of the idea and proposed developing a "smart course," sometimes known as an adaptive learning course. Smart courseware has the ability to know students and the way they learn. It "remembers" what a student has accessed on-line (for example, charts, lectures, and resources). It also recognizes the speed at which the student learns, what courses have been completed, grades on all materials, and preferred professors—in short, the unique learning style of the student. Smart classes link evaluation and assessment to instruction and content in a closed circle.

This professor had just authored a paper about this general idea. To provide a national platform for this kind of reform, the head of ETC contacted his former colleagues at the College Board to talk about developing this technology-mediated model biology course. They were keenly interested. The grants officer decided that this idea was an appropriate request for the Fund for the Improvement of Postsecondary Education (FIPSE). Recognizing FIPSE's requirements in regard to assessment of projects, the director of institutional research became an active member of the proposal development team. Her involvement and focus on the outcomes of the project led to a clearer expression of the project's goals, and thus the proposal became stronger. Her ideas for assessing the program helped everyone see how to improve the implementation of the program in the light of the goals and objectives. She also talked with FIPSE's evaluation expert before finalizing her assessment plan.

The final assessment plan was built around the two overriding goals of the program: (1) strengthening and deepening students' understanding of biological facts and principles and (2) improving students' awareness of their own approaches to learning. To address the first goal, the evaluation called for the College Board's Advanced Placement (AP) biology exam to be given at both the beginning and end of the course. In addition, a questionnaire was to be designed and administered that asked students about their perceptions of self-improvement in their understanding of biology. To address the second goal, a questionnaire was to be designed and administered that determined the types of learning activities the students used during the course. A qualitative component included interviews of students and faculty. Data are to be collected in each of the three years of the project, with the first year being dedicated to collecting baseline data before the changes in the course are fully implemented. The desired outcomes are for students exposed to the technology-mediated course to exhibit a better understanding of biology, as well as a better understanding of their own successful approaches to learning.

The grant was awarded, and the project directors have been developing the course. At the same time, the director of institutional research has been implementing certain portions of the assessment plan. In particular, she has designed the two questionnaires. They were constructed as Web forms by a staff member of the ETC and are being piloted with students taking introductory biology. The director of institutional research will then refine the questionnaires as well as the mechanism for administering them. The director has also conducted some focus group interviews of students taking introductory biology in order to gather the qualitative and contextual information about ways in which students learn. The project directors have been working with the biology faculty to be sure that the AP biology exam has been given at both the beginning and end of the semester. Most important, all of those involved in the grant—the project directors, the director of institutional research, the director of corporate and foundation relations, and the biology faculty—have met to talk about the progress being made. This communication is vital as a way to keep people focused on the goals of the grant and ensure that data gathered as part of the assessment are talked about as the project continues to be developed.

This kind of feedback on a specific project encourages faculty to create new, wider feedback loops with momentum for systemic change. The assessment process has contributed to keeping teaching ideas fresh and responsive to students' needs. Once this kind of momentum for change using evaluation is set in motion, it sustains itself and can lead to continual improvement of teaching and learning. The idea of assessment has become more natural to our project directors on this grant, and this shift in attitude toward assessment may lead to wider institutional change. Most important perhaps, having data to support project outcomes has helped the faculty directors and the top levels of administration, including the dean for academic affairs and the president, to see its impact on student learning.

CHRISTINE BROOKS COTE is director of institutional research and registrar at Bowdoin College, New Brunswick, Maine.

MARIANNE JORDAN is director of corporate and foundation relations, Office of Capital Support, Bowdoin College.

PART THREE

Investing in Science Education

9

A clear understanding of why to invest in faculty and how must be an integral part of the strategic planning process.

Investing in Faculty

Project Kaleidoscope, Core Institution Task Force

If the efforts to achieve strong undergraduate communities in STEM are to be sustained, colleges and universities must give attention to policies and practices that affect all facets of institutional life, from admissions standards to graduation requirements, curricular planning to campus planning. In the process of setting forth an institutional vision, primary attention must be given to the character and quality of the faculty. A clear understanding of why to invest in faculty and how must be an integral part of the strategic planning process.

We are convinced that as much diligence is necessary to realize a return on the capital investment made in people as to realize an appropriate return from an investment in a plant; thus, we submit that it is essential to look at costs related to faculty not simply as a critical expense, but as part of an intentional investment strategy meant to produce an important and significant value-added benefit.

Supporting costs incurred in building and sustaining a strong faculty (individually and collectively exemplars of the scholarly tradition) should be part of a larger institutional budgeting and investing strategy. A decision to award tenure is a capital investment of about $3 million, more than an idle commitment. Because significant long-term resources have been committed, there must be an accompanying commitment on behalf of the institution and faculty alike to ensure the highest and best use is made of that investment.

These investments must cover both fixed and nonfixed asset costs. Fixed asset costs, those most often considered in the budgeting process, are substantial over the life of a faculty member. An investment over the thirty-year life of a science faculty member (whose initial base annual salary is between $45,000 and $60,000, augmented with an average 3 to 4 percent cost of living adjustment) totals close to $3 million. Institutional salaries differ, but the premise is still pertinent.

What is not often considered in the strategic planning process is the nonfixed asset investments in STEM faculty. Opportunities to make nonfixed asset investments are numerous, including those for additional and differential merit awards and recognition for achievement, leadership development, scholarly growth and renewal opportunities (for example, leaves, sabbaticals, workshops, mentoring, and internal reassignments), and a range of infrastructure needs.

A preliminary analysis suggests that very modest nonfixed asset investments are needed to ensure that the fixed asset investment will reach its full potential. On average, nonfixed asset investments range between $200,000 and $500,000 over the life of an average science faculty member; this is only 20 percent of the fixed asset investment, but still a critical expenditure. Again, the character of scholarly activity expected and supported by different institutions will have an impact on the extent of such investments.

Failure to provide the necessary support (nonfixed asset investments) throughout a career is not a realistically cost-effective or sensible investment strategy for colleges and universities seeking to build and sustain strong programs in mathematics, engineering, and the various fields of science. Experience demonstrates that a productive return on this modest nonfixed asset investment can make the difference between maximum productivity and returns (as measured in student learning outcomes, quality of scholarly productivity, and societal service) and more modest returns on the initial investment made through fixed asset costs. In many instances, nonfixed asset investments are proportionally greater in pretenure years, as institutions direct more attention to this stage of faculty careers. In the posttenure period, where institutions make 80 percent of the overall fixed asset investment in faculty, the trend is toward only about 10 percent investment in the nonfixed assets portion. This is puzzling.

Key investments made at different career stages can affect the return on an investment in faculty, especially if it is understood that faculty at all career stages have responsibility for remaining current in their discipline and visibly active in their scholarly community and providing access for all students to a rigorous and captivating engagement with mathematics and the various fields of science.

An Investment Road Map

Consider where and how to invest in faculty from the point of recruitment through the pretenure years. The first step is to recruit faculty who meet the mission of the program and institution and then, in the process of hiring, to clarify departmental expectations for long-term success in the departmental and institutional context and set forth clear and well-articulated measures of success.

Consider the nonfixed asset costs at this stage, which can include:

- Establishing physical infrastructure to support research activity
- Providing mentoring opportunities
- Providing support for pedagogical development
- Reducing teaching loads for pretenure faculty
- Reducing service expectations in the first year
- Providing a pretenure leave program, possibly competitive, to undertake full-time research or gain new pedagogical or technical expertise.

Colleges and universities must develop policies and practices that recognize the long-term contribution that each individual faculty member makes to the education of students and the service of the institution over the long term. Thus, the same attention and support should be available for midcareer and senior faculty as for faculty at the pretenure stage.

Regular interviews concerning institutional expectations must continue for faculty at all career stages with the chair, deans, mentors, colleagues, and others. Requirements for recognition and reward, promotion and tenure must be developed and promulgated widely. Sabbatical leave programs exist, with faculty held accountable for articulating both their professional needs for a leave and how that professional leave will make a return on the institutional investment.

Support must be available to explore and initiate new approaches in research and teaching—for example:

- Internal small grants programs for pilot and high-risk projects
- Internal endowment funds for faculty renewal efforts
- Administrative structures and personnel to advise and facilitate career planning
- Staff support for nonfaculty duties in laboratories
- Centers for faculty development and improvement of teaching
- Internal funding opportunities, mentoring programs, proposal writing workshops, and internal retooling grants
- Laboratories, offices, and equipment adequate to pursue scholarly endeavors
- Travel to professional meetings and workshops related to research and teaching.

Ways to Finance This Investment

Securing resources adequate to make a critical investment of faculty at all career stages requires instituting policies and practices to use current resources in a more targeted fashion, reallocating existing resources, and increasing designated gifts and grants.

Strategic planning must recognize investing in faculty as a priority of the institution, not merely an item on the cost side of the budget. This must then lead to an appropriate allocation and reallocation of resources to meet those expectations. Periodic evaluations of resource allocations must be made to ensure that expenditures have the greatest impact on faculty careers and institutional goals. Early planning and institutional conversations must occur if operational funds are needed and if development campaigns are to support new and increased investments. Such conversation should consider:

- Multiyear rather than annual budget planning
- The expectation of three- to five-year faculty career plans
- Faculty grants, technology enhancements, and capital equipment matching funds as standard budget items
- Establishing endowments for program elements outlined in this investment strategy

Strong and continued interactions between development officers and faculty must be encouraged. The development office must be included in the planning process for programs and must work with faculty (and vice versa) in proposal writing and alumni outreach effort. Faculty should be expected to write proposals to secure external support for their individual scholarly needs, as well as for departmental and institutional needs.

Assessing the Return on an Investment in Faculty

There are several means by which to measure the return on investment in faculty:

- High retention of vital and committed faculty results in continuity and continued strengthening of the program, and recognition of quality programs brings distinction to the institution.
- Visibility as an institution of distinction aids in attracting and retaining subsequent generations of good faculty.
- Visibility attracts increasing support from alumni, foundations, extramural agencies, industries, and others, and strong faculty are more competitive in the search for external support.
- Good students are attracted, admissions and retention go up, and the bottom line is strong.

Because of all this, the institution enjoys increasing distinction and market share and is able to provide a better education to students, who then become satisfied alumni. There are equally beneficial returns on a carefully targeted investment in faculty—for example:

- More productive use of resources (including time)
- Identification of nonproductive expenditures of limited resources
- A growing sense of community as agreement about common goals and the means to achieve those goals

- An increased level of trust between the institution and faculty built on clearly communicated expectations
- A recognition of distinctiveness that comes with visible commitment to building and sustaining a strong faculty in the context of institutional mission and identity and changing societal needs

If the assessment reveals that the current investment strategies are not achieving desired (or desirable) goals, then institutions must be creative and tenacious in realigning resources so that goals are met. To visualize a strategy, one must understand that it is the institutional strategic planning that leads to financing strategies. Financing strategies then identify funds for investment from several places, including operating budgets that receive

Exhibit 9.1.   Worksheet to Determine the Cost of Investments to Sustain Quality Faculty

Salary Considerations
Initial Salary: _____ increased at ____ % per year for ____ years = _____
Pretenure Dollars (insert figures for first six years):   _____
Posttenure Dollars (insert figures for remaining years):   _____

Enrichment and Renewal Considerations
Pretenure
  Recruitment   _____
  Start-up Costs   _____
  Internal Development Grants   _____
  Release Time (include replacement costs)   _____
  Travel (six to seven trips during
  the pretenure period)   _____
  Special Development Costs (e.g., scholarly
  and professional development meetings,
  mentoring programs)   _____
  Pretenure Sabbatical Costs (if appropriate)   _____
  Matching Grant Costs (calculate for one or
  more grants as appropriate)   _____
  Other   _____
    Subtotal (pretenure)   _____

Posttenure
  Released Time (include replacement costs)   _____
  Sabbaticals (include replacement costs)   _____
  Matching Grant Costs (calculate for two or
  more grants as appropriate)   _____
  Travel (scholarly and professional development
  trips)   _____
  Retooling Costs   _____
  Other   _____
    Subtotal (posttenure)   _____

TOTAL (noninstitutional expenditures):   _____

money from gifts and grants, endowment income, partnerships and joint ventures, and tuition and fees. Because raising new funds through sponsored projects and fundraising for current and capital expenditures, cost increases, and partnerships are strategies already being pursued at most institutions, it may be that significant restructuring and reallocation are in order. The process for anticipating costs of nurturing faculty at different career stages can be determined using templates like the one in Exhibit 9.1.

THE PKAL CORE INSTITUTION TASK FORCE, supported by a grant from the U.S. Department of Education and Fund for the Improvement of Postsecondary Education, documents the progress of nearly forty colleges and universities in institutionalizing and assessing new approaches to strengthening the environment for learning.

10

Learning and teaching centers serve as repositories of institutional memory and catalysts of campus conversations about critical educational issues.

Learning and Teaching Centers: Hubs of Educational Reform

Susan R. Singer

As we approach the thirtieth anniversary of perhaps the first formal learning and teaching center (LTC), the University of Michigan's Center for Research on Learning and Teaching, it is timely to both celebrate and examine the role of such centers in educational reform. A quick review of the mission statements and histories of centers at small and large, public and private institutions reveals a complexity of goals, strategies, and customization specific to each institution. The shared thread is a strong commitment to enhancing learning and teaching excellence. Cross (2001) noted that establishing LTCs has been the most common approach nationwide to improving teaching and learning. The Center for Teaching Excellence at the University of Kansas has links to over 220 LTC Web sites in the United States and more for LTCs abroad (http://eagle.cc.ukans.edu/~cte/resources/websites/unitedstates.html). This extensive list is not exhaustive. In addition, many new LTCs are being launched. We can celebrate about a three-hundred-fold increase in LTCs in the past thirty years. Arguably, the two most significant contributions LTCs can make to educational reform are (1) maintaining high-visibility, high-credibility, campuswide conversation focused on forward-looking learning and teaching and (2) providing quality support for all teachers, from beginning instructors to experienced, highly regarded faculty members.

Where Have We Been?

Not only have LTCs appeared on more campuses in the past three decades, but the nature and visibility of these centers on campus have increased. The major shift in emphasis has been from remedial to leading-edge teaching.

Federal, private, and university funds have been directed toward faculty development since the 1970s to help faculty improve their teaching. After the 1962 establishment of the University of Michigan's center, the next milestone was the Danforth Foundation's grants in 1975 to five institutions (Empire State College of the State University of New York, Harvard, Northwestern, Spelman, and Stanford) to establish LTCs. This funding lasted until 1978 when the perpetual problem of sustaining grant-supported initiatives had to be faced.

Northwestern's Center for the Teaching Professions, established in 1969, used Danforth funding for a faculty development program aimed at thirteen liberal arts colleges in the Midwest. In 1992, an endowment from the Searle family established Northwestern's Searle Center for Teaching Excellence. The Searle Center offers high-quality teaching workshops for faculty as a small piece of extensive on-campus programming and support. Stanford and Harvard used Danforth funds to establish LTCs that continue today with other funding sources. The initial audience was graduate teaching assistants, but that later expanded to include faculty. Stanford's Danforth funds were also used to promote the improvement of teaching in higher education regionally. Today, Stanford continues to reach outward with Rick Reis's Tomorrow's Professor listserv: "Desk-Top Faculty Development, One Hundred Times a Year" (see http://sll.stanford.edu/projects/tomprof/ newtomprof/postings.html). The Stanford University Learning Lab, like Harvard's Web site, provides a broad array of information on teaching valued by many at other colleges and universities. The Harvard-Danforth Center for Teaching and Learning, established to enhance undergraduate education, is now the Derek Bok Center for Teaching and Learning. Empire State College and Spelman continued to support faculty development but did not form LTCs.

By the 1990s, LTCs on many campuses provided the resources for faculty orientation, mentoring programs, peer support groups, individual consultations, workshops, seminars, resource libraries, and newsletters (Graf, Albright, and Wheeler, 1992). LTCs at primarily undergraduate institutions became more visible in the 1990s. One of the first, Carleton College's Perlman Center for Learning and Teaching, was founded in 1992 with support from the Bush Foundation. Sustainability was ensured when Lawrence Perlman later endowed the center. The formalization of such centers at both small and large institutions has increased campus conversations on learning and institutional cross-fertilization of ideas. Campus visits and communications among institutions that are forming centers and those establishing centers disseminate best practices.

Professional organizations, including the Professional and Organizational Development Network in Higher Education (POD), American Association for Higher Education (AAHE), and Association of American Colleges and Universities, facilitate the exchange among a broader audience and creatively move reform ahead on a larger scale. Many research societies have become actively engaged in educational reform in the past decade. At the national level, organizations like Project Kaleidoscope began broadening the conversation about effective teaching and learning among disciplines, in this case science, math, and engineering. Locally, LTCs play a crucial role in integrating and disseminating information about educational reform to and from the campus community. Travis (1995) stressed the need for both local faculty development and broader dissemination of effective practices. Some LTCs have become models of effective local implementation of educational reform and national disseminators. Fledgling LTCs appear to gain momentum in part from the diversity of LTCs that have emerged over the past thirty years.

Where Are We Today?

LTCs today share a common assumption that excellence in teaching and learning is attainable with support, information, and practice. This assumption has been validated by the work of Boice (1992, 2001), Travis (1995), and others. LTCs continue moving through a process of professionalization, especially with the continued growth of POD. Advances in cognitive sciences applied to learning and a growing body of literature on the multiple dimensions of learning are key to the increased value of LTCs to the constituents they serve.

Metaphorically, an LTC is the hub of a wheel with many spokes. Information flows in and out of spokes that are context specific. Some centers have thematic foci, for example, technology (University of Delaware, Rensselaer Polytechnic Institute, and American University) or writing (Duke University's Center for Teaching, Learning, and Writing). Others focus on developing future faculty through major reform in graduate education, including the preparation of teaching assistants. The resources that Graf, Albright, and Wheeler (1992) describe continue to be strong elements of many centers that have continued to mature and be reshaped by experience and ongoing research. Some programs, such as Carleton's, include a student observer program. This program pairs a faculty member with a student who observes and discusses the class with the faculty member but is not enrolled in the course. As with other LTCs, faculty consultation is also available. Some centers are beginning to explore the scholarship of teaching (Hutchings and Shulman, 1999), while others focus on helping faculty find synergies between their disciplinary scholarship and teaching. An example of the latter is Macalester College, where the Center for Scholarship and Teaching is being launched.

Programs for new faculty may well be the most instantiated in the core of LTC activities, underscored by the recognition of the tremendous investment institutions make in new faculty (see Chapter Nine, this volume). Mentoring programs, extended orientations, and workshops for new faculty can ease the transition into an academic career and presumably enhance learning for students of new faculty. LTCs have long recognized the importance of supporting all phases of a faculty member's career. Indeed, midcareer faculty renewal may have been the initial impetus for early programs. Posttenure faculty development is being reexplored at many institutions (Alstete, 2000). A recent emphasis on meeting the unique needs of faculty at pivotal points in their career has been leveraged, in part, by Mellon grants to clusters of institutions. The collaborative nature of these grants parallels the increasing exchange of information about learning and teaching among institutions.

The growing number of LTCs and the increased participation by faculty at all ranks in LTC programming provide evidence that conversations are occurring. Unfortunately, such conversations are not occurring at all institutions or within all departments at an institution. Are faculty and future faculty better prepared and supported in their work because of the increased LTC activity? Informal surveys and evaluations of LTCs indicate this is likely. Research by Boice (1992, 2001) and others supports the conclusion that programmatic activities can strengthen faculty teaching effectiveness. LTCs provide and sustain such programming in many colleges and universities. Rice, Sorcinelli, and Austin (2000) interviewed 350 faculty member in the AAHE Heeding New Voices study, which confirmed several best practices recommendations for new faculty, including using LTC resources and mentoring programs. This paper contains an exceptionally helpful bibliography on mentoring, as well as teaching and research development programs.

The most important question to address is whether student learning has been enhanced as a result of LTCs. As Ratcliff, Johnson, La Nasa, and Gaff (2001) note in an AACU summary of a national survey, "Assessment of complex learning goals remains an aspiration rather than a reality in many institutions" (p. 18). Investigating links between student learning and LTC activities is an even more complex challenge for this decade.

Organizational barriers and flawed strategies for implementation present significant barriers to reform (Ratcliff, Johnson, La Nasa, and Gaff, 2001). LTCs offer one organizational strategy with great promise for educational reform. Mullin (2001) claims that no revolution, which he defines as a quantum change, has occurred in undergraduate education in thirty years. His major concern is that educational systems have not changed and rely heavily on a course credit model for measuring academic progress. He calls for a systemic change exemplified by Alverno College, where grades and course credits have been replaced with ongoing learning assessment system. It is an all-or-none approach and discounts incremental institutional change. I would argue that the smaller-scale revolution LTCs are bringing to campuses has moved us forward in meaningful ways. LTCs foster an environment where a controversial claim like Mullin's can be constructively discussed and smaller-scale challenges for faculty members can be addressed. LTCs have a growing track record of steady education reform, and the trajectory for the future is exciting.

Where Are We Going?

The academic career of a faculty member is markedly different today than it was thirty years ago (Rice, Sorcinelli, and Austin, 2000). LTCs will need to be flexible and visionary to meet changing needs. Integrating and applying new findings in the learning sciences to curriculum development is an important way LTCs can serve their institutions. Asking whether curricular innovations are enhancing student learning is becoming increasingly possible. LTCs need not become assessment centers, but can certainly serve as liaisons between faculty innovators and resources for designing and implementing assessment of programmatic or curricular reform efforts.

Technology and pedagogy interfaces are becoming increasingly complex. LTCs can bridge explorations of appropriate technologies and effective technologies to enhance learning among faculty, information technology specialists, and librarians. On the horizon are virtual learning and teaching centers with the potential to complement the work of physical centers and include a broader net of faculty in the ongoing work of educational reform.

LTC coordinators also have a role to play as faculty at colleges and universities search for synergies or balance between their scholarly pursuits and commitment to teaching excellence. The professoriat is being redefined in many ways, and LTCs can take a lead in Rice's call in *Making a Place for the New American Scholar* (1996). Real educational reform requires sustained high-quality efforts. The physical presence of LTCs on campus lends credibility and support to the mission of maximizing the learning of all students. As repositories of institutional memory, coordinators of campus conversation on learning and teaching, and part of larger national and international conversations on education, LTCs maximize the forward momentum of educational reform

References

Albright, M. J., and Graf, D. L. (eds.). "Teaching in the Information Age: The Role of Educational Technology." New Directions for Teaching and Learning, no. 51, San Francisco: Jossey-Bass, 1992.

Alstete, J. W. *Post Tenure Faculty Development: Building a System of Faculty Improvement and Appreciation.* San Francisco: Jossey-Bass, 2000.

Boice, R. *The New Faculty Member.* San Francisco: Jossey-Bass, 1992.

Boice, R. *Advice for New Faculty Members.* Needham Heights, Mass.: Allyn & Bacon, 2001.

Centra, J. A. *Faculty Development Practices in U.S. Colleges and Universities.* Princeton, N.J.: Educational Testing Service, 1976.

Cross, K. P. "Leading-Edge Efforts to Improve Teaching and Learning." *Change,* 2001, 33(4), 31–37.

Graf, D. L., Albright, M. J., and Wheeler, D. W. "Faculty Development's Role in Improving Undergraduate Education." New Directions for Teaching and Learning, no. 51. San Francisco: Jossey-Bass, 1992.

Hutchings, P., and Shulman, L. S. "The Scholarship of Teaching." *Change,* 1999, *31*(5), 10–15.

Mullin, R. "The Undergraduate Revolution: Change the System or Give Incrementalism Another Thirty Years?" *Change,* 2001, *33*(5), 54–58.

Ratcliff, J. L., Johnson, D. K., La Nasa, S. M., and Gaff, J. G. *The Status of General Education in the Year 2000: Summary of a National Survey.* Washington, D.C.: Association of American Colleges and Universities, 2001.

Rice, R. E. *Making a Place for the New American Scholar. New Pathways.* Washington, D.C.: American Association for Higher Education, 1996.

Rice, R. E., Sorcinelli, M. D., and Austin, A. E. *Heeding New Voices: Academic Careers for a New Generation.* Washington, D.C.: American Association for Higher Education, 2000.

Spence, L. D. "The Case Against Teaching." *Change,* 2001, *33*(6), pp. 10–19

Travis, J. E. *Models for Improving College Teaching: A Faculty Resource.* San Francisco: Jossey-Bass, 1995.

Wright, D. L. "Faculty Development Centers in Research Universities: A Study of Resources and Programs." *To Improve the Academy,* 2000, *18,* 291–301.

SUSAN R. SINGER is professor of biology and Humphrey Doerman Professor of Liberal Learning in the Department of Biology and Perlman Center for Teaching and Learning at Carleton College, Northfield, Minnesota.

11

Mission statements at the departmental level can frame strategic planning and assessment efforts, build community, and focus teaching and research activities.

Linking Departmental and Institutional Mission

J. K. Haynes

A top priority for the members of the biology department at Morehouse College is creating a research- and a resource-rich environment for learning. A major objective is to engage most of the students in research and increase the number of well-prepared students who pursue graduate studies.

In 1989, department faculty revised the biology curriculum. Three new required courses were added ("Plant Sciences," "Ecology," and "Senior Seminar," a capstone course), along with a requirement that student majors take three laboratory courses beyond "General Biology." In addition, a sequence of three elective courses in research was introduced.

This was a significant change in our curriculum, and thus, early in the process, we decided to develop a mission statement for the department. "Specialization: The Enriched Major" in Ernest Boyer's book, *College: The Undergraduate Experience in America* (1987), helped in developing the mission statement. The process of bringing this statement to life made us think as a department about the breadth of the educational experience that students should have, as well as about the role of research in the department.

The mission statement we arrived at frames our strategic planning and assessment efforts and reminds faculty old and new on a daily basis why we are here. Extracurricular student development activities are consistent in both spirit and priority with goals in the mission statement. It is widely posted around the department and provides an incentive for faculty and students to function as a community working toward achieving goals that have been embraced by all.

Most important, the department mission is consistent with and supports the overall mission of the college. It seemed clear from the outset that department goals that were not aligned with institutional goals were unlikely to be achieved and were probably not worth achieving in the first place.

There were a number of objectives that we wanted to capture, two of them paramount: to provide students with a broad understanding of the field of biology and to assist in developing their creativity and reasoning skills. Both objectives are essential to the mission of liberal arts colleges like Morehouse. We believed that providing students with opportunities to do inquiry-driven laboratory experiments in teaching laboratories and the research laboratories of faculty members was an important mechanism to achieve these ends. Yet a number of barriers had to be overcome in developing a mission statement that we could agree on and would serve students well.

Based on this experience, the following guidelines in developing a mission statement are recommended:

- Involve all faculty members in the department in the process and also solicit student input.
- Know the mission of the college, and seek to reinforce as many of the college's goals as possible.
- Adopt reasonable goals that are congruent with department resources.
- Make clear to all involved in developing the mission statement that it is a living mission, subject to change on annual review.
- Develop an assessment plan that includes measurable objectives and performance indicators.

Today, the mission statement is discussed regularly throughout the academic year and is included in department publications and posted on bulletin boards throughout the department, as well as discussed during freshman orientation with biology majors. Students thus have a better understanding of what we expect of them. A side benefit is that the mission statement and attendant planning and assessment have brought us closer to being a community of scholars than before.

Following is the mission statement the department developed:

Mission of Morehouse Biology Department

The mission of the department is to:

- Provide students with a fundamental knowledge of biology
- Prepare students for and assist them in entering the work force and graduate and professionals schools.
- Strengthen the reading, writing and quantitative skills of our students.
- Develop the analytical reasoning and creative thinking skills of our students—expose students to contemporary research techniques in biology and enhance their understanding of the scientific method.

- Conduct meritorious research, within this community, in the field of biology.
- Acquaint students with the history of biology, including the contributions of Black biologists.
- Engender an appreciation among our students of the social and economic implications of discoveries in biology.
- Build the awareness of our students of the ethical and moral issues related to basic tenets in biology.

This mission provides a framework for the student support programs that we have developed, as well as grants for extramural support. Based on it, we have established a national program in the summer for high school students interested in research careers. We have also developed a weekly seminar series that brings leading scientists to our campus to talk about their work and interact with students.

A key component of the Morehouse biology experience that derives directly from the mission statement is our program of mentoring students. Many students are mentored by faculty members while serving as research assistants, tutors, and teaching assistants. In addition, there are three career counseling offices associated with the department that in addition to providing counseling, also provide opportunities for students to serve as apprentices to professionals in areas of their career interest. The career counseling offices sponsor a number of activities that provide extracurricular support for our overall program. For example, the research careers office sponsors an annual research symposium at which students in all science disciplines give poster presentations and a research club that sponsors talks by scientists and visits to science facilities.

The sense of community is significantly more visible than in the past. Departmental committees for curriculum, facilities, and grants are more active and focused. The involvement of students as colleagues in research is greater. We have a far more integrated counseling apparatus, funded by external grants, to help students make the link from campus to graduate school or the world of work.

As we continued to work through translating the mission into action, we began to realize some gaps in our work. We had not clearly enough established a detailed assessment plan that was linked to departmental goals. We did not have in place performance evaluation measures, assessment tools, or procedures to document outcomes and impact on student learning. We have started that process. Departmental Goal 3, for example, states:

To enhance research activity we have established the following objectives, outcomes, and performance evaluation measures:

Objectives

To increase research productivity of departmental faculty

To increase student participation in research

Outcomes
    Increased faculty research funding and publications
    Increased numbers of student research publications at scientific meetings
Performance Evaluation Measures
    Each faculty member with a research laboratory will hold at least one research
    grant and publish at least two refereed articles per year.
    Each faculty member with research students should have at least one student
    present his research at a meeting each year.

Several years ago, the college began an assessment program that ties curriculum planning to college mission and budget. Each department is required to submit an annual assessment report to a collegewide assessment committee, which indicates its success in achieving annual goals (milestones in a five-year comprehensive plan) and the plan for the following year. This report is transmitted through the office of the vice president for policy and planning, who reviews it to ensure that the information is complete and in the appropriate form. The assessment council, which consists largely of faculty members, reviews individual plans to see how reasonable they are based on assessment data and department and college goals, and it then submits an evaluation and recommendation to the vice president for academic affairs. This person then holds discussions and engages in negotiations with department heads before submitting recommendations to the budget and strategic planning committee. This committee reviews recommendations from the assessment council and vice president for academic affairs and makes budget adjustments based on strategic imperatives at the college. By and large, departments that are successful in achieving their goals and planning will be rewarded in their budget allocation for the next academic year.

This plan, which couples department planning with collegewide planning and budgeting, should put teeth into the effort to make departments take planning and assessment far more seriously than at present. We have more to do, but our experience might be helpful to other departments.

Reference

Boyer, E. *College: The Undergraduate Experience in America.* New York: HarperCollins, 1987.

J. K. HAYNES is dean of the Division of Science and Mathematics at Morehouse College, Atlanta, Georgia.

12

Imagining new spaces for science can be a defining moment in the life of an institution, as the campus community addresses fundamental questions about how a major investment in science facilities is an investment in the future of their college or university.

A Perspective on Campus Planning

Arthur J. Lidsky

Every day, college and university campuses change—usually imperceptibly and occasionally dramatically. Programs change, people change, financial resources change, buildings change, land and landscapes change, environs change. The way campuses look today is the result of all the minor and significant, casual and formal, rational and irrational decisions that are made in the day-to-day dynamic interaction of a living institution responding to such changes. The impetus for new construction of college and university buildings in the 1950s and 1960s was increasing enrollments and expanding programs. Today, the forces for change on campuses are a myriad of complex issues—for example:

- Changes in the academic disciplines
- An increase in and awareness of interrelated disciplines
- Decreased federal and state funds for programs, operations, research, and facilities
- Increasing awareness of environmental issues and concerns—"green architecture" and campus design
- Increasing competition of for-profit institutions and on-line programs
- An increasing interrelationship of business, industry, and educational institutions
- Increasing numbers of faculty and students (including undergraduates) involved in research at both the university and college level
- Increasing federal and state regulations and standards for life safety and building safety
- Increasing use and sophistication of instrumentation, computers, and various presentation and communication media

- Pedagogical changes such as an increasing effort to involve students in the process of learning by doing—experiential learning
- Student consumer shopping for the college of his or her choice
- The ticking time bomb of deferred maintenance

Given all these forces, colleges and universities must plan deliberately, carefully, and rationally. Planning must become a fundamental and underlying theme woven tightly into the day-to-day operations and interactions of the institution, whatever its type. The future health of higher education depends on better planning and management. The planning process described in this chapter is necessarily generic but can be tailored and shaped to fit the needs and circumstances of all.

Campus planning is the process of identifying and guiding those institutional decisions in higher education that have spatial implications. The responsibility of academic leaders, it is a process of guiding the development of a campus so that it supports functional, aesthetic, and economic goals within the context of an institution's history, mission, and vision for the future.

There are today over four thousand colleges and universities in the United States; they differ by mission, academic objectives, and program emphasis. Enrollments range in size from several hundred students to more than fifty thousand students. The institutions differ from the perspective of numbers of faculty and staff; fiscal and physical resources, including levels of endowment; and forms of governance. And today we must add the for-profit category to this taxonomy.

However, higher education is more complex than that simple differentiation of public, private, and for-profit suggests. The taxonomy can be expanded to include residential and commuter and institutions with national, regional, and local focus. Even that taxonomy is too general, for institutions can be further described as urban, suburban, or rural; a city college, state university, land- or sea-grant institution, research university, liberal arts college, or community college. The definitions can be expanded to include coed, male, female, religious, military, and historically black. Some can be further refined, for example, by subject: business, law, or engineering.

Conceptually, the campus planning process can be divided into different components that are addressed sequentially, iteratively, or concurrently (Figure 12.1). Although these steps for planning are generic and can be used in a variety of contexts, for institutions seeking to build and sustain strong undergraduate programs in mathematics and the various fields of science, this comprehensive planning process is crucial. Maintaining strong programs in these fields is a costly endeavor, over the short as well as the long terms. Institutional leaders, who must make decisions about using resources prudently and creatively, have to decide at every step about the cost of decisions made and those not made. For the number of students involved, the costs of maintaining strength in these STEM fields may appear disproportionate, particularly in comparison to other departments with higher enrollments. However, as science and technology have an increasing impact on all life and work, colleges and universities, and those leading them, have a responsibility to make a rigorous encounter with these fields an integral part of the undergraduate curriculum for all students.

The advice that follows outlines considerations for trustees, presidents, and other academic leaders in early stages in considering making a major investment in facilities that support learning, teaching, and research in mathematics, technology, and the various fields of science and engineering.

Figure 12.1. Campus Planning Process

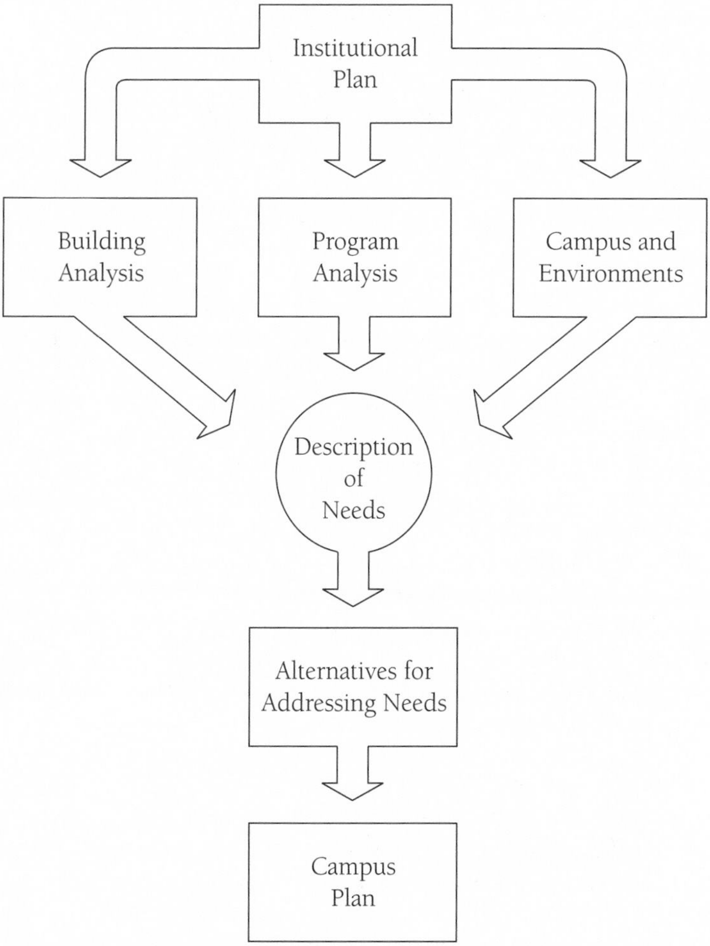

Source: Dober, Lidsky, Craig and Associates, 2001.

Institutional Plan

There are five interrelated elements of the institutional plan: mission statement, academic plan, staffing plan, capital budget plan, and the operating budget plan. Of the five, the academic plan is the most central, but without a solid statement of mission in place that outlines a vision of the institutional future, there should be no final decisions made about the academic plan. This is because there must be a campuswide understanding about how building and sustaining strong programs in science and mathematics connect to the institutional mission. However, once academic planning is underway and guided by the mission statement, it becomes the pivotal element.

An academic plan should have a point of view about programs and curriculum, about enrollments and staffing, and about programs that will grow, remain constant, be reduced or eliminated, or nurtured as special resources. All other institutional planning will flow from the goals, objectives, and priorities of the academic plan. On many campuses, building consensus and reaching closure during the academic planning process will take several years.

Building, Program, and Campus and Environs Analysis

Following or coincident with institutional planning is an institutional audit of the physical infrastructure: an assessment of the existing buildings, campus, infrastructure, and environs. Here generic questions about spaces and the physical infrastructure need to be asked:

- How much space does the institution have to support its mission and academic plan today and into the future?
- Are the amount, condition, configuration, and use of space appropriate?
- Are the spaces sufficiently flexible to support programmatic change over time?
- Are the buildings capable of sustaining network, media, and communications improvements?
- What are the critical spatial relationships and patterns of interactions?

This analysis of campus and environs usually consists of some combination of an assessment of building location and use, land ownership, open space and landscape, pedestrian and vehicular circulation, parking, topography, and utility infrastructure. In some instances, a detailed infrastructure analysis is conducted prior to or as a separate part of the campus planning study.

The analysis then moves to an assessment of the academic programs relative to campus resources in terms of the degree to which those spaces and environs support current and planned changes in learning, teaching, and research. In the context of making decisions about serving a mission and academic plan that focuses on strengthening student learning in fields of mathematics, science, engineering, and technology, questions such as the following need to be asked:

- How many faculty, students, and staff are there today, and how many will there be tomorrow?
- What is the level of research activity expected of those faculty and of the engagement of undergraduates in that faculty research?
- What is the nature of each department's pedagogy? What new approaches are being considered?
- What will be in the impact of technologies in undergraduate learning?
- How will the pedagogy change, and do the physical resources help or hinder the program?
- What are the critical programmatic affinities?
- Are new interdisciplinary programs anticipated?
- Is there to be an increase of students engaged in learning these fields?

Description of Needs

The goal of this analysis of facilities, program, and campus is to provide a foundation for developing a description of precise facilities needs required to support the mission and academic plan. Needs may vary from minor staffing requirements or cosmetic changes, to improvements that may involve renovating or adding to an existing building, to the construction of an entirely new building. Campuses with different missions and identities will arrive at a distinctly different set of needs, but at institutions of all types, the grounding question for this analysis should be, What difference will this make to our efforts to strengthen student learning?

Developing this list of needs, like attending to the mission statement, must be through a participatory process involving a broad spectrum of the community. A key objective here is consensus; however, the list of needs must not be a wish list reflecting individual wants and desires. Comparisons with peers, the use of standard guidelines, and the application of best practices can play a role in keeping the what are viewed as needs in line with reality. (This is a point at which academic leaders must be certain that they and their faculty colleagues are connected to colleagues beyond their campus, aware of the achievements of others pursuing similar educational and institutional goals.) Each item must be carefully vetted and justified in the context of the institutional mission and the consensus in regard to the academic plan. Finally, agreement should be arrived at in regard to priorities from that list, and this agreement document should be publicized widely. This is particularly important in considering the major financial investments that are probable if new spaces for science are to take shape. The entire campus community must buy into the need, and this will happen only as they are convinced that addressing these needs serves the larger institutional mission and goals.

Alternatives for Addressing Needs

Once there is agreement on needs and priorities, campus leaders can explore alternatives for addressing the needs. Some alternatives might be operational: a change in the way in which rooms are scheduled, for instance, or the sharing of sophisticated instrumentation and equipment. Other alternatives may relate to the physical infrastructure, with little visible impact on the campus, while others may have significant impact on open space, circulation, aesthetics, and the campus as a whole. If this becomes the option, leaders will have to make decisions that address the domino effect that happens on a campus when a major improvement or new construction is considered.

Facility alternatives can vary in scale; they can be some combination of reallocated space and relocated functions requiring minor renovation, significant renovation, the construction of new space added to a building, or the construction of a new building. If a building has historic significance, restoration could be a major factor. Short-term solutions to nagging problems may surface at this stage, and leaders must be alert to this. Arriving at new spaces is ultimately an extended process, and some needs (student gathering spaces, more technological connections, classrooms with chairs on wheels) can be addressed quickly and at modest cost.

For many, this stage of the planning process is the most enjoyable and most exciting. New ideas and possibilities are explored. Large portions of the institution's community come together in small and large groups to discuss possibilities. The possibilities seem endless, but they are not. Just as the preparation of the list of needs should be done to avoid a wish list, alternatives should be categorized by the degree of feasibility and necessity. The difficult part of this phase of the planning process is the selection of criteria against which the alternatives will be measured and judged. Criteria could include factors relating to construction, project, and operating costs; timing and phasing; the extent to which the alternative meets programmatic requirements; the extent to which the alternative meets specified spatial relationships and design goals; the extent to which the siting of a new building enhances the overall campus design; and so on.

An important reason to give serious attention to a wide range of alternatives is that as the project proceeds, unanticipated difficulties and opportunities will surface (for example, not enough funds, an unexpected gift, a new faculty appointment with research interests not served in planning). By having a wide range of alternatives already on the table, you will be better prepared to keep the project on schedule.

The Campus Plan

Once the assessment of alternatives is complete, emerging from a broad-based, widely participatory process, a campus plan begins to take shape. Often during this process, new alternatives have risen, and others begin to connect in new ways. Finally, through fiat or consensus, one set of alternatives is chosen to address the defined needs and priorities. This then becomes the campus plan.

Since implementing all the elements of the campus plan at once is usually impossible, campus leaders must set priorities to accomplish projects over a defined time period, say, ten to fifteen years. Most campuses reevaluate projects—and their costs and benefits—after five to seven years. Based on the needs and assumptions at that time, the plan is either confirmed or modified to reflect current realities.

Campus plans are usually summarized with graphics and text. Often the audience is both internal and external. For the college or university community, the plan is a record of the process, analysis, needs, alternatives considered, and the plan itself. External audiences can be state offices responsible for funding or other governance entities, as well as potential donors.

The planning documentation will include sections on context and background, a description of the existing situation, a description of the analysis of current building and campus, and an outline of programmatic initiatives and needs based on the institutional plan. There will also be a visual presentation of the campus plan, with a bird's-eye view to illustrate the intention; there will be preliminary determinations about phasing and implementing the plan, along with the estimates of costs to be associated with each stage.

Conclusion

Planning gives institutions an opportunity to ask fundamental questions about mission, program, fiscal resources, facilities, and environs. To be effective, planning must be participatory and involve those who will be affected by the plan: students, faculty, staff, and the community. Planning becomes the framework for addressing those questions in an integrated, open, and rational process.

A campus ultimately is an expression of its mission and educational philosophy. It reveals understandings about the relationship between how and what and where students learn. Those of us involved in this aspect of Project Kaleidoscope over the past decade have come to see how the planning of new spaces and structures for science can be a defining moment in the life of the institution. In this planning, decisions are made that give evidence of how a particular college and university is responding to the contextual changes: serving all students, infusing the learning environment with the excitement of discovery, and accommodating new directions in science.

References

Keller, G. *Academic Strategy*. Baltimore, Md.: Johns Hopkins University Press, 1983.
Millett, J. "Relating Governance to Leadership." In P. Jedamus and M. W. Peterson (eds.), *Improving Academic Management: Handbook for Planning and Institutional Research*. San Francisco: Jossey-Bass, 1980.

ARTHUR J. LIDSKY *is president of Dober, Lidsky, Craig and Associates, Belmont, Massachusetts.*

13

Technology-driven transformations of the learning environment are here to stay, and there is no alternative to precise planning to ensure that they serve larger institutional goals over the long term.

Investing in Digital Resources

David McArthur

The basic reason that today's leaders of institutions of higher education should plan for and invest in e-learning is simple: to make the best use of emerging technologies to enhance existing methods of learning and create new ways to fulfill their core teaching and learning missions.

It no longer makes sense to debate whether e-learning should be accepted or rejected—either in individual schools or by higher education as a whole—just as it is no longer reasonable to consider spurning the Web in business or at home. At best, such debates lead to profitless diatribes or to a Luddite-like resistance to new productivity technologies. At worst, they distract academic leaders from dealing with the challenges surrounding the effective selection and deployment of the e-learning alternatives that will serve their students and their campus best.

Planning for e-learning is critical. When it is done right, the campus will be able to:

- Involve technologies as an avenue to embellish the student-faculty and student-student interactions that are so integral to a quality undergraduate experience.
- Improve faculty satisfaction by implementing an on-line resource center for instructional resources.
- Develop Web-based programs to increase enrollments.
- Scale up infrastructure and support services to incorporate and use technologies more effectively within its academic program.
- Enhance the preparation of students in ways that make them more competitive applicants in the work environment.

NEW DIRECTIONS FOR HIGHER EDUCATION, no. 119, Fall 2002 © Wiley Periodicals, Inc.

The recently coined term *e-learning* is intended to encompass all these approaches. Under this broad umbrella of practices, academics have begun to identify and classify different e-learning variants in ways that capture their similarities and differences better than earlier terms.

A Definition

It will be helpful to define what I mean by e-learning. When the idea of distributing educational materials on the Web was relatively novel, about the late 1990s, phrases such as *distance education* and *on-line learning* could be used more or less interchangeably. As practices have matured, it has become clear that these terms confound a number of distinct ideas and educational delivery options, only a few of which might entail learning without face-to-face contact with instructors, or getting educated at a distance.

Table 13.1 outlines a set of Web-instruction definitions that Collegis, which provides business, technology, and curriculum services to colleges and universities, uses when outlining the varieties of e-learning alternatives. In the progression from Web displayed to fully on-line, more and more of the essential activities in teaching activities make use of the Web, and as this happens, learning becomes at least potentially freed from constraints of time and place.

None of these e-learning options necessarily diminishes the role of the instructor in learning and teaching. This is, of course, a natural assumption to make, since a fully on-line course can often be taken by students in a self-directed manner, with little or no faculty interaction or support. But there are varieties of e-learning opportunities that engage both learner and teacher as colleagues in the same space. Relatively few of the e-learning courses we have helped develop over the past several years have been designed as self-directed learning opportunities or, to reduce costs, as ways to reduce the number of face-to-face instructor contact hours. It must be clear to those planning that most e-learning in higher education has nothing to do with digital diploma mills or automating education. It has everything to do with creating an environment in which students can shape and own their personal learning with appropriate ease and flexibility.

Why Plan

But even as individuals and institutions experiment with the range of types of e-learning described in Table 13.1, it is clear that skeptics and critics are right about one thing: e-learning, like other technology-driven transformations, is easy to do badly. Some of the failures are spectacular and newsworthy, but far more costly to higher education in the aggregate are the hundreds of small experiments with e-learning on campuses across the country that start as grassroots efforts and have led nowhere. As Bill Graves,

Table 13.1.   Web Instruction Definitions

Type Description	Example
Web displayed	The classroom is used for face-to-face engagement between teacher and learner. The Web presents on-line syllabus, readings, and assignments; there is no Web-based communication with instructor or with peers. An instructor who has taught a freshman calculus course for years decides to put her course outline and assignments (already in digital format) on a Web server managed by the university. Links to readings that are available on the Web are also provided, a digital supplement to the printed course pack. Class times and schedule are unchanged from previous semesters.
Web enhanced	In addition to the components for Web displayed, this may also include on-line lectures and interactions that include chat or threaded discussion, as well as some assessment. The classroom is still the main physical space for learning. A professor of Romance languages uses a course management system to put all materials and assignments for a course on-line. Face-to-face lectures remain the main delivery vehicle. However, assignments are organized around threaded Web discussions, and summarization of these on-line conversations counts for half the course grade.
Hybrid	Uses all Web-displayed and Web-enhanced components; however, on-line content and interaction have been increased, and Web-based assessment and feedback replace or enrich some class sessions. A semester-long graduate-level course meets on a regular schedule for the first three class sessions and then moves on-line for class discussion, team problem solving, and independent assignment submission on a regularly scheduled basis. At the end of the semester, the class meets for final presentations and a final examination.
On-line	There is no face-to-face component in this learning experience. Interaction, feedback, assignments, and other characteristics of Web-displayed and Web-enhanced courses are used to engage students. This shift does not necessarily imply less involvement by the faculty member. A course is fully on-line, with students starting every week and completing the course within twelve weeks. Students take the course from any location and do not interact with one another, but an instructor is available for questions. In addition, students participate in a current issues on-line discussion forum at least once during the course.

Source: The typology is taken from one that originated with Anne Parker, vice president for strategic consulting services at Collegis.

founder and CEO of Collegis says, there are far too many random acts of progress and far too few plans for campuswide e-learning growth. The constructive reaction to these problems is not to toss out e-learning as a passing fad but rather to tackle it as a challenge that demands careful institutional planning.

Some major problems confront systemic planning for e-learning. First, although there are numerous technology options available to colleges and universities, only a few of them may be appropriate to serve the identity and mission of a particular campus. And, second, although many institutions adapt technologies with the intent of enhancing their existing mission, e-learning is a disruptive technology: it encourages universities to consider both radical alternatives as well as those that might change a school's goals and vision only incrementally.

Schools that have begun to take e-learning seriously are doing so because they are taking on a number of hard issues: fresh competitors; new business models; different student populations, programs, or markets; innovative ways to transform educational experiences; and methods of keeping costs under control. But the clear lesson learned from the experiences of these campuses is to begin not by focusing on the technological options—they are, after all, only tools—but rather by converging on a clear vision of where the university or college wants to go and then consider that vision in the light of new options and the institutional goals they enable.

Even when colleges find a satisfying vision in the large set of e-learning alternatives, that is just the beginning. It is more demanding to go from that vision to a tangible plan and then to the implementation that leads finally to a sustainable (and evolving) e-learning presence on the campus. This is the kind of effort that is described elsewhere in this book in thinking about investing in facilities or faculty. And just as in those planning arenas, what complicates the series of steps to develop and realize a coherent e-learning plan is that it rarely can be done hit and miss, by individuals here and there across the campus.

As Project Kaleidoscope has recognized, to achieve successful change, institutions and their leading agents of change must put all the puzzle pieces together in concert. Views differ as to exactly what these pieces are in the realm of e-learning. However, when first assessing the institutional readiness to launch an e-learning venture, institutions must consider at least six critical success factors:

- The current capacity of the university's network and computer infrastructure
- The understanding, vision, and willingness of the institution's leaders to underwrite change
- The current or potential availability of resources, both people and dollars
- The commitment to faculty development
- The sophistication of the management and planning structure
- The availability of on-line services for students

Each of these pieces needs to be firmly in place if an institution is going to achieve a sustainable, systemic, or institutionwide e-learning success. Attending to all of these factors is a time-consuming and expensive process for colleges and universities. Most schools (large and small) would find it impossible to build a new campuswide intranet, maintain instructor training for a growing number of faculty who are going on-line for the first time, and keep a help desk for students staffed around the clock while at the same time meeting all their other obligations to students and faculty. Rather than taking this systemic approach, it is often cheaper and easier to simply let motivated and technically savvy instructors build on-line courses as their time permits. This is practical in the short term, but it is not a formula for long-term scalable e-learning success. Fortunately, it is not the only approach; there are others that are affordable and lead to change that is sustainable over the long term, serving the institutional mission well.

What to Do

A couple of broad practical points are worth noting for developing and implementing cost-effective strategic plans for e-learning in higher education.

Staged Implementation. Although schools should attend to the critical factors associated with e-learning in a coordinated way, this does not mean all the pieces have to be fully implemented at the same time. It does make sense to start with a thorough strategic planning exercise that encompasses all the factors and to stage the implementation phases. Exhibit 13.1 suggests one effective way to sequence on-campus activities. Some tasks clearly must precede others; for example, trainers who can share their expertise on course management systems (CMS) with other instructors effectively must have already completed CMS training. Some services are continuous; examples are a student and instructor help desk. Others recur at regular intervals, for example, quarterly planning updates. And yet others, such as instructional design consultations and course development services, may be revisited and deepened several times (and perhaps should be) as an institution gains a better understanding of where it wants to go with e-learning.

This kind of staging helps institutions choose the right service at the right time and can reduce the overall cost of developing and implementing an e-learning environment that works for the campus. By trying out new on-line courses and tools on a small scale and then assessing the results, universities can limit the risk of investing too early in services only, to realize much later that plans are not working effectively or are inconsistent with their evolving missions.

Appropriate Outsourcing. Staging the implementation of far-reaching e-learning plans is prudent, but by itself this approach is unlikely to have a dramatic effect on cost containment if higher education institutions provide all the services internally. Some schools, for example, lack the scale to justify providing their own infrastructure support, yet their students and instructors will need around-the-clock network services and always-available

Exhibit 13.1.   Sequencing On-Campus Activities for e-Learning

	Year 1				Year 2				Year 3			
Strategic Services												
Initial e-learning readiness/status review	▓											
E-learning vision and strategic plan	▓	▓										
Distance learning organizational and financial plan		▓										
Student administrative services for e-learning												
Instructor development plan				▓								
Course management system selection			▓									
Market analysis		▓										
Quarterly planning updates					▓	▓	▓	▓				
Annual outcomes evaluation report					▓		▓		▓			
Infrastructure Support Services												
24×7 Student and Instructor Technical Help Desk	▓	▓			▓				▓			
24×7 high-bandwidth, redundant global network	▓		▓		▓				▓			
24×7 client-branded CMS server	▓		▓		▓		▓		▓			
Site coordinator training		▓			▓				▓			
Instructional Development Services												
Instructional design help desk for trained instructors	▓	▓			▓		▓		▓			
CMS training	▓											
E-learning pedagogy for trained instructors	▓											
Train the trainers	▓	▓										
Mentor training program		▓	▓									
Instructional design consultation services						▓				▓		
Course development services		▓				▓				▓		
Instructional materials acquisition and integration					▓	▓						
Web Integration Services												
e-learning technology integration plan					▓							
e-learning technology integration implementation					▓	▓						

Source: Collegis.

help desk services as their e-learning implementations get off the ground. Indeed, the importance of these services is likely to be most critical during the earliest—and smallest-scale—phases of e-learning. For such schools, outsourcing of at least some e-learning services is essential, not optional.

Larger universities enjoy the economies of scale that enable them to provide e-learning services in-house. Many schools can keep a large information technology staff very busy providing faculty training and support, as well as help desk services. Of course, at some point, all schools outsource. Even the biggest schools are not in the business, for example, of laying and maintaining fiber-optic cable; these basic networking services are best left to partners such as MCI or AT&T. Furthermore, for large schools and small, outsourcing is becoming increasingly attractive, as it is for businesses in general, because the Internet, which delivers much e-learning content, has greatly reduced the transaction costs and frictions of coordinating with external partners.

For instance, faculty who get help in building their courses through on-line chatrooms or asynchronous forum discussions often do not know, and do not care, that this service is being hosted by third-party experts at remote server installations rather than on campus. All this means that even universities that are large enough to sustain their own full-time help desk, instructional designers, consulting expertise, and training services can often save greatly by outsourcing them. (See Graves, 2000, for more on the "Law of the Virtual Campus".)

The closer a service comes to the core missions of the institution, the more reluctant colleges and universities are to outsource services, regardless of how much money can be saved (Heterick, 2001). Hardware-related networking services, for instance, have been happily farmed out by higher education institutions, primarily because they are have never been viewed as a critical part of their educational or research mission. Pedagogical expertise, on the other hand, is widely regarded as an educational core asset, so outsourcing of equipping the community with the skills to use on-line course tools effectively is a tougher sell. This is understandable, but it raises several hard questions. When is a service too close to critical missions to outsource? And because outsourcing often saves money, how much are schools willing to pay to keep services in-house?

Colleges and universities will have to answer this for themselves, because each has a different view of its mission. A few innovative schools, such as the Kentucky Virtual University, have taken outsourcing completely to heart. The small staff (fewer than twenty) see their mission as selecting and aggregating courses (developed by other partner schools in Kentucky), marketing, and ensuring the quality of student services. All other traditional higher educational services are outsourced to partners including Collegis (hosting, infrastructure support, professional training, and course development), Cambridge Technology Partners (software implementation), and the Kentucky Community and Technical College System (student information system operation). Such examples aside, however, higher education has been much more reluctant to outsource than other industries. Over the past decade, many businesses have reorganized, cut back services to include only core competencies, and partnered with other firms to provide a complete package of services for customers. For many in higher education, abandoning the "not-invented-here" attitude is coming much more slowly.

This reluctance is not surprising. Most institutions of higher education, until recently protected from market forces that typically spur change, have had few incentives to outsource. Perhaps more to the point, such conservative attitudes cannot simply be thrown out. Rather, they need to be replaced with sensible alternatives—ones, we think, that should derive from a strategic plan for e-learning.

References

Graves, W. "The Law of the Virtual Campus." *Educause Information Resources Library.* [http://www.educause.edu/asp/doclib/abstract.asp?ID=NLI0013]. 2000.

Heterick, R. The Outsourcing Paradox. *The Learning Market Space.* [http://www.center .rpi.edu/LForum/lm/Sept01.html]. Sept. 1, 2001.

DAVID MCARTHUR *is a senior consultant for Collegis, Inc., in Morrisville, North Carolina.*

PART FOUR

The Perspectives of Leadership

14

Systemic reform of undergraduate science and mathematics education requires that faculty innovators and administrative leaders work together.

The Variables of Positive Change

Daniel F. Sullivan

Systemic change requires an institutionwide strategy. What distinguishes efforts at institutionwide reform from course and curriculum development, which is also important, is that this reform is about systemic change, and systemic change requires an institutional strategy. Systems are groups of variables linked together organically. The links are not simple linear, sequential, cause-and-effect relationships. There are positive and negative feedback loops, and the system is dynamic. (It is clear where the kaleidoscope metaphor within Project Kaleidoscope came.)

One must come to think of one's own institution as a system. A strategy for systemic change must involve all the relevant institutional variables, and all or most of them must be in play pretty much from the start. Sometimes it feels like pushing several large rocks up hill simultaneously, and it is.

In addition, local opportunities and barriers matter a great deal; the local details, in fact, are critical. Building on successful models from other institutions is helpful and necessary, but science education reform always involves local adaptations of more general strategies, not simply the dissemination of packets of success from one institution to another. Communication and sharing are critical, especially at the level of strategy and exemplification, but no institution can acquire a module from elsewhere and just install it. It has to adapt what it sees working elsewhere to its particular circumstances or invent solutions, in partnership with faculty and others on campus. Local resource constraints and historic commitments require different trade-offs from one institution to another, and the details of campuswide politics introduce other opportunities and constraints. However, it should be noted that most common problems are being addressed somewhere and that the most expeditious and cost-effective approaches over the long term are to identify, build on, and adapt reforms initiated in other settings.

Systemic change takes time. The institutions I know that are making the most progress have been at it for a long time. A significant increment of change can take five to ten years precisely because many variables must be in play simultaneously. The system itself is complex.

Institutional strategies should build on existing strengths and involve faculty and administrative partnership. Systemic change is most possible when there is a strategic science or mathematics education strength in the institution that can be built on. In all institutions I have visited, ranging from those with the highest reputations to those that are struggling, I met at least some faculty who understood how to do undergraduate science and mathematics education well and who seemed to have the capacity, with appropriate support, to get things going in the right direction. Finding a source of bottom-up leadership that can be joined with institutional leadership is a key to successful change.

For a great many years, the national approach to improving undergraduate science education was primarily, though not exclusively, to encourage and then respond to individual faculty initiatives. If there was a national systemic change strategy, I believe it was to create a critical mass of change agents at institutions by supporting strong, inventive, and entrepreneurial faculty one by one. If and when a critical mass was achieved, the thinking went, institutionwide reform would be under way, and it would also be sustainable. The premise was that this would work because faculty are around for a long time, while presidents and deans change with remarkable frequency. A better strategy is to focus on the faculty.

In many instances, this strategy paid off handsomely. Initiatives begun in some institutions as far back as the late 1960s and early 1970s are now the foundation stones of today's reformed and reforming programs, sustained at least partly by the now-mature faculty who received initial federal support many years ago.

Yet it is clear that the colleges and universities that have come the furthest in science and mathematics education were those where faculty innovators and leaders were joined by senior administrative partners to pursue together—institutionally—the ideas faculty had for doing science and mathematics education better. Presidential and top-level administrative leadership is a critical multiplier of faculty efforts. In fact, I do not believe that real institutionwide reform can happen without strong partnerships between administrative and faculty leadership.

Administrative leadership, critical when the quality of science and mathematics departments is strong, is also critical when programs are uneven or faculty leadership is unevenly distributed across departments. Long term, there is no substitute for shaping a faculty of the best quality one can manage, having a compelling institutional vision, and tuning the faculty reward system so that it encourages faculty to do the right things. In the shorter term, for systemic change to happen, presidents and deans must find in the faculty those who are ready to move and place strategic bets. Again, partnerships are key.

Paradoxically, having significant facilities and technology needs can be a wonderful boon to systemic change. One thing we have learned is that getting facilities and technology right is critical to getting change to happen; conversely, if facilities and technology are barriers to effective teaching and learning, change is very hard. Bucking facilities that are improperly conceived to support learning communities eventually wears faculty down, and they give up, even when highly motivated to do the right things.

The old architectural maxim, "We shape our spaces and then they shape us," is nowhere truer than in science and mathematics education. When teaching spaces have been designed for the traditional lecture, recitation, and lab format, it is difficult, if not impossible, to do studio teaching or to teach intensive, combined lecture-lab courses where students spend more of their time doing science. It is also difficult to take advantage of the high leverage on student learning that the use of technology can provide, especially in courses with students organized in groups for collaboration in learning—the way much science research is conducted. Furthermore, for student-faculty research to thrive, there must be spaces thoughtfully planned and set aside for that purpose. Thus, any serious attempt at systemic change must include a local commitment to assess the state of facilities and technology and then to ensure that spaces and technology support the new approaches to student learning desired.

When an institution has facilities needs it must address, its leaders have an unusual amount of leverage on the other players who must be a part of systemic change. Because significant amounts of capital must be raised to address science space needs—among college and university facilities, they are the most expensive—the attention of everyone in the institution is drawn to the teaching and learning issues at stake. The process of facilities programming and design can be a wonderfully strategic vehicle for forcing the extensive conversations systemic change requires. I believe, therefore, that although other factors are important, institutions seeking systemic change in the sciences are lucky if they have major facilities problems to address.

The existence of real facilities and technology needs in an institution often looks like a barrier to most college and university leaders precisely because they know such investments will be costly, and because they see themselves as lacking the ability to raise capital easily. I do mean to say, however, that a strategy of systemic change that ignores the facilities dimension is inadequate. At whatever level the institution can afford, a facilities improvement plan must be a part of the strategy of systemic change.

Understanding the local institutional cost structure of science and mathematics education is important if cost is not to become a barrier to reform. This discussion of facilities leads naturally to the issue of the cost structure of undergraduate science and mathematics education. If systemic change is to happen, it is critical to make a careful study of the cost structure of the system devoted to science and mathematics education in each institution. The reconfigured science education system sought must be financially attainable and then financially sustainable. Study of the cost structure may show that changes initially thought to be too expensive may be quite affordable. Or it may turn out that change in science and mathematics education may be possible only if trade-offs are made against other possible institutional educational goals, something that is frequently tough to manage. One thing we know from experience is that absent clear evidence that a reformed system is both financially attainable and then sustainable, key institutional players will block reform.

In the vast majority of colleges and universities, systemic change in science and mathematics education will not be possible without comprehensive, multiyear, combined operating and capital budget financial planning. It is continually surprising to me that so few institutions engage in this kind of planning. In both the independent and public sectors, failure to achieve overall institutional financial equilibrium will create an institutional climate antithetical to the kind of boldness of imagination, risk taking, and new investment necessary for institutionwide systemic reform. This is not the place to rehearse this argument in detail.

What is important here is to reinforce how important overall institutional planning and financial equilibrium are to the accomplishment of systemic change in science and mathematics education. It can happen only in the context of a larger institutional plan, which is necessarily a part of each local strategy of systemic change.

An important benefit of the required change to new accounting standards is that we must look much more frequently now at total institutional financial health when we examine our numbers. It has been my experience that when one begins to look at one's institution in this new way (new to us, old to our trustees from for-profit corporations), degrees of financial flexibility (and sometimes financial weakness) emerge that are hidden when we examine ourselves only in a fund accounting mode.

One place where such financial planning can produce important benefits is in the purchase and maintenance of capital equipment, an area that often produces great frustration among science and mathematics faculty. Major pieces of equipment are frequently too expensive to afford with funds available in one year's operating or capital budget. But if one approaches science equipment funding on a three-year basis, planning for lumpy expenditures and spreading them out over departments to smooth overall cash flow, departmental planning can be stabilized, and it may become possible to purchase items inconceivable in any other way and without outside grant support. This mode of budgeting for capital equipment purchases also maximizes the opportunity that faculty and the administration together have to seek outside support to supplement institutional funds. Savvy foundation officers look both for an understanding on the part of the institution of the need to include equipment costs, not just construction costs, in facilities plans and for institutional commitment to support science education intelligently over the long haul. An equipment acquisition plan is one important kind of institutional commitment.

A global look at the cost structure of science and mathematics education may also include the discovery of positive financial consequences from improved student retention. When introductory science and mathematics courses are pumps and not filters, good students not only stay in science and mathematics longer; they also tend to drop out less frequently. Some institutions capture this positive effect through improved admissions selectivity (when there are fewer students to replace, fewer applicants need to be admitted initially), leading to a stronger market position, with its impact on net tuition revenue. Others achieve it through lower annual student recruitment costs, though this is very hard. Still others capture it through higher enrollment spread over the same fixed cost base. Although such positive financial benefits are clearly possible, they are hard to predict and therefore hard to build into a multiyear financial plan. Nonetheless, there are many institutional examples of this kind of effect.

Getting the introductory courses right is absolutely critical. This is an old insight that continually bears repeating because things are still not right with the introductory courses: systemic, institutionwide reform in science and mathematics education cannot occur if the introductory courses are filters. At most institutions, the introductory courses still need the greater near-term attention. This is true regardless of whether the students go on to science and mathematics majors or whether they are destined to major in the arts, humanities, or social sciences and the goal is just science literacy. In my experience, the institutions that have come the furthest in undergraduate science and mathematics education reform have begun by improving their introductory courses with real passion.

My experience teaches that careful thought needs to be given to what happens if systemic reform is really successful. One must pay attention to the possibility of a whole range of unintended consequences. Student recruitment patterns may be dramatically altered, with consequences for both nonscience departments and science departments. On many campuses that have strengthened their programs, the percentage of incoming freshmen planning to major in natural science or mathematics increases significantly. As learning science becomes more attractive to prospective students, more and better ones apply for admission and are accepted, and more of those accepted enrolled. At the same time, current students were more satisfied and took even more science courses. How could anything be wrong with this picture?

If enrollments in nonscience courses decline as a consequence of a dramatic increase in the attractiveness of science courses, there will be serious institutional curricular planning issues, increased political opposition among nonscience faculty to further (or continue) investments in science education, and a decreased willingness among faculty in nonscience departments to collaborate with science faculty in interdisciplinary teaching. At the same time, even when an institution is able to increase the numbers of science faculty, such increases always lag enrollment growth and are never proportional to enrollment growth. The pressures on science faculty increase dramatically as a result of their success, and burnout among the best faculty becomes an issue. Thinking through these possibilities ahead of time is crucial.

Improving institutional capacities to assess learning outcomes, and therefore to evaluate the impact of attempted reforms, is essential, as is fine-tuning the faculty reward structure so that it is in line with the direction of planned reforms. Without changes in the reward structure, reform will not happen. A research-rich environment for students cannot be created unless even the faculty at undergraduate colleges and universities without a research mission are supported as they seek to do research appropriate to the setting. It is impossible, in my view, to expect students to learn how to ask good questions, analyze, and be lifelong learners with the intellectual curiosity of the educated person if faculty members are not also expected to model these qualities.

These are some of the things I have learned through experience in my time as a liberal arts college leader of undergraduate science and mathematics education reform. My recommendations are practical and applicable to a wide variety of institutional settings exemplifying a different mix of resources, strengths, constraints, and opportunities—the realities that institutional leaders face in their day-to-day efforts to move their institutions forward. The work of institutionwide systemic reform of undergraduate science and mathematics education is critical to institutional health and the future of our students and our nation.

DANIEL F. SULLIVAN is president of St. Lawrence University, Canton, New York.

15

A key player in the institutional effort to build and sustain strong undergraduate STEM programs is the grants officer, who knows where and how to secure the external gifts and grants essential to accomplishing strategic initiatives.

The Role of the Grants Officer

Lee W. Willard

Just as the profiles of faculty careers change and develop over time, from young assistant professors to tenured scholar-teachers and experienced senior mentors, so do those of institutions. As colleges and universities recruit excellent faculty, attract talented students, and develop innovative courses of study, they strengthen their core missions and gain external credibility. Presidents, provosts, and deans bear the responsibility of promoting progress along this institutional continuum no less than do chairs of individual faculty. Grants officers are essential partners in this enterprise. Indeed, it is no small coincidence that the doors above the offices of grant writers, donor cultivators, and funding specialists often bear the titles "development" or "institutional advancement," for grants officers have central roles to play in this vital and dynamic process.

Securing external support is not optional for institutions. With increasing pressures to hold down undergraduate tuition, escalating competition for faculty, pressing needs for state-of-the-art facilities, and the growth of information and instructional technology, colleges and universities must become increasingly competitive and successful in extramural fundraising. Such efforts are necessary not only to respond to new ideas and initiatives but also to sustain the traditional core and substance of the institution. Indeed, successful fundraising is one indicator of an institution's health and vitality. It signals internally, as well as externally, that the college or university has a clear sense of itself; that it is playing in the local, regional, or national scene; and that its story and mission merit the support of alumni, other donors, and funding agencies.

Some colleges and universities have experienced staff and dedicated offices to support grant and development activities; others must rely on presidents or individual faculty members for program and proposal development. But regardless of configuration, any institution can be successful if it is willing to engage in the enterprise and see development activity as an integral and regular part of academic and faculty activity. Indeed, faculty and students are often the best spokespersons for the institution. Moreover, success leads to success. A junior faculty member may be talented and lucky enough to win a small internal grant or young investigator award; the receipt of that individual award may make his or her department more competitive with an external course and curriculum or facilities grant. Several departments with curricular or facilities grants may then make the school or college more competitive for state, corporate, or foundation funding. An array of corporate and foundation funding, in turn, may make the institution eligible for national invitational programs and nominations. Successful national projects lead to additional funding possibilities—and so it goes. Small efforts are important in and of themselves, and they lay the foundation for credibility and future success, establishing a rhythm of institutional growth and development. Thus, the work of individuals who share an educational vision and are willing to venture into these endeavors can make a tremendous difference in the life of an institution.

Grants officers are instrumental in this process; they are at the same time goad and glue. As goad, they are institutional planners and shapers and catalysts for change, and they force dynamic dialogue. As glue, they create linkages and consensus, marshal resources, strengthen the sense of institutional identity, and develop common purpose. In short, they help the institution find its common ground and channel its institutional voice.

The first and most obvious key function of the grants officer is of assimilating funding information and interpreting national trends. By reading annual reports of foundations and corporations, researching funding directories and databases, and meeting with alumni and other donors, the grants or development officer develops insight into the themes and issues of particular interest to particular funders—for example, inquiry-based learning, diversity and cross-cultural inquiry, civic engagement, or technology and society. This insight is particularly important because while faculty may frequently be willing to engage in development or grants-seeking efforts, they seldom have the knowledge of what particular funding source to target or what tack might be most productive. The grants officer can serve as a critical institutional interlocutor, translator of national trends and the higher education context.

Another key function relates to intrainstitutional knowledge and memory. By meeting and getting to know faculty and administrators, reading campus newspapers and publications, attending talks, and chatting with students, grants officers come to know the exciting—and fundable—initiatives within the college or university. They garner anecdotes, quotations, and examples that make proposals come to life and prove authentic. Moreover, grants officers are readily able to see commonality among departments and programs and to introduce groups across campus and help them work together. Armed with this knowledge and expertise, they can better match faculty and projects to funding possibilities. Perhaps equally important, they can advise what is unlikely to be funded, saving faculty energy and institutional expectation.

Grants officers also act as institutional planners, sometimes intentionally and at other times inadvertently. In provoking response to funding initiatives and donors, thinking through the institutional rationale, and creating and describing mechanisms for program implementation, grants officers of necessity become institutional planners. Not only do they articulate what the institution wants to do; sometimes the institution does what the grants officer articulates. This interconnection between institutional development is apparent in the following outline for a proposal structure that could just as well be a template for an institutional planning effort:

- Goals. Where do we want to be? What do we value? What do we want to do?
- Needs. Why does this need to be done?
- Capability. Do we have the right institutional experience? Expertise? People involved?
- Timeliness. Is this the right time? What is the current status of the institution?
- Plan. How will we do this?
- Resources. What do we need? What do we have?
- Significance. What difference will it make? How will we know if we have succeeded?

The role of the grants officer is not a simple one or easily or cleanly delineated: facilitator, instigator, interpreter, writer, planner, and more. What is clear, however, is that these roles are interrelated and increasingly important to the health and vibrancy of colleges and universities.

LEE W. WILLARD is associate dean for academic planning and special projects, Arts and Sciences and Trinity College, at Duke University, Durham, North Carolina.

16

Leadership at the divisional level helps to form and frame a sense of community that breaks down disciplinary boundaries, encourages the joint pursuit of a research-rich learning environment, and fosters the scholarly career of each member of the faculty in the context of serving broader institutional goals.

The Role of the Science Dean

James M. Gentile

The process of reform at Hope College has been the steady, unyielding commitment to a vision of a research-rich environment for learning by faculty and administrators alike. A key position here in exercising that commitment has been that of the dean of natural sciences. The dean not only serves as the administrative head of a set of related programs but also is the key individual at articulating divisional needs and perspectives to senior administrators at the institution, as well as helping faculty gain insight on issues facing institution as a whole. This allows for perspectives to be shared by all parties in all directions and ensures that decisions (whether they are made by senior administrators, the dean, chairs, or faculty members) are always made within the broader institutional and divisional context.

Setting Divisionwide Goals

It is the responsibility of the dean of natural sciences to work with departmental chairpersons to sharpen individual programmatic goals and objectives and, more important, provide overarching direction within the division. This is so that all departments are pointing in the same direction: aware and supportive of the vision and direction articulated by other departments within the division and how these departmental visions serve the division as a whole. The dean helps to form and frame a sense of community and an agenda for action for the division. This focus on direction influences how we hire faculty, socialize faculty into our community, and pay attention to faculty at all career stages. It shapes our attention to the physical infrastructure, as well as our agenda for programmatic change. An example is found in the interplay that has occurred over the past five years relative to our understanding of our divisional programmatic vision, how we could move toward accomplishing that vision, and how our physical environment must be shaped to support and extend that vision.

We started out with discussion and conversations about how to break down the silos of department structures so as to form better bridges for students and faculty to interact with one another at the fuzzy boundaries where scientific thought and insight overlap. Many faculty members were reluctant even to engage in the conversation. Old turf battles came to the fore, and fears of change abounded. Other faculty eagerly sought a venue for conversation that was open and did not give appearances to anyone that a coup was being undertaken. As dean, I provided the "food" solution: a "free lunch and free conversation" zone was established, a place in which any faculty member (and any administrator) could leave all baggage at the door, share food with one another, and discuss what a new approach to student learning in science and mathematics at Hope College might look like.

At first, as few as five faculty (out of a potential pool of sixty-five) attended. Interest grew, and within a year, about thirty faculty routinely attended these divisional lunches, with about fifty of the total pool of faculty in the division coming at least occasionally. The result was a new core curriculum for students not majoring in science, one that is distinctively interdisciplinary and hands-on and in which mathematics is integrated with, rather than segregated from, science teaching and learning. These lunches continue to this day, with topics of conversation changing, but with the key outcome of a community of scholars interacting with one another in a nonthreatening manner and having the ability (and encouragement) to develop their own agenda for conversation.

A second result from this effort was the initial planning for a new science building. From the very first conversations about need, every individual with a stake in the effort was at the table. The dean of science was asked to play the lead role, and faculty, students, institutional administrators, key staff personnel (administrative assistants, janitors, maintenance engineers, groundskeepers), alumni, and trustees became engaged in the discussions, the planning efforts, the selection of an architectural team to undertake the project, and intimate details of putting a physical reality to a programmatic vision and need. The outcome is ownership by all of a significantly interdisciplinary space in which faculty scholarship and teaching, and student research and learning, will take place, as well as an architectural masterpiece that will add a center of excellence to the campus community as a whole.

A true community in science and mathematics has evolved at Hope over the years. As with any other community, there are disagreements and differences of opinion about the how reform will take place; nevertheless, the faculty members are unified in a common vision for hands-on learning and research experiences for all students.

Faculty work together on a host of issues, including curriculum design, campus research needs, outreach programs to the K–12 community, and exporting the vision to the world outside the campus through proposal writing, participation in professional associations, and publications.

Nurturing Faculty and Staff Careers

An agreement that the departments and division are pointing in the same direction is the foundation for thinking about careers of faculty in our division. We all recognize that individuals within a department and within the division as a whole can assume different roles, depending on their professional agenda and the larger departmental and institutional needs now and into the future. Faculty members with demanding research programs are given ample time to conduct their work with students in research laboratories because those faculty without current student-centered research programs willingly assume extra teaching and minor administrative responsibilities. This ensures the research productivity of their colleagues, as well as the overall integrity of our program. Other faculty take on major responsibilities for curricular development and are encouraged by colleagues for their leadership in this critical area of institutional life.

Departments collaborate in allocating regular time during the week for all colleagues to engage in scholarly activities. The responsibility of the dean is to know the needs and dreams of each individual faculty member and to work with him or her, together with other divisional leaders, to ensure that the greatest potential is achieved from each of the scholars within our division.

On our campus, such a commitment means we identify and recruit only those highest-quality scholars who can articulate and embrace the overall vision for excellence in teaching and research that is fundamental to our mission and contribute to the distinctiveness of our program. This can mean that even when the search process yields a pool of excellent individuals, it may not necessarily include individuals appropriate for our institution. The willingness to extend searches as long as necessary to select the right person is a cost in real dollars, as well as in time and energy.

Investing in People

Other costs relating to early career faculty are for the research start-up costs that are essential if these faculty are to be productive colleagues within our community of scholars. Our approach is simple. The significant start-up costs, which include a one-course release in the first year, are accompanied by the expectation that a major request for external support be one product of that released time. That this is an investment with significant return is revealed many times, when the external grant award received is significantly more than our initial support and sets the faculty member up in a research program for several years. The process of proposal development during the first year has benefits beyond the new faculty member. Each entering member of the Hope science faculty is mentored, informally and formally, by colleagues, some within and some beyond the department. Thus, ideas from graduate school, an industrial experience, or another academic institution have easy entry into the discussions on our campus. Perhaps this could happen without the administrative structure of the dean of natural sciences, but probably not as effectively.

We also pay important attention to the professional development of individuals who hold staff positions in science and mathematics at Hope. These individuals are keys to our success, and their satisfaction with and growth in their jobs go a long way to building and sustaining the broader community that defines our programs. For example, laboratory coordinators in all departments are encouraged and expected to attend faculty meetings so that their voices can be heard and they can better understand tasks that they will have to undertake. Travel monies for staff members are provided so that they can further their own intellectual and professional development.

Another example exists within the office of the dean. The executive assistant to the dean, in a role similar to that described for laboratory coordinators, attends all divisional chairperson meetings and has an active voice in conversations about programs and needs. Her insights bring a well-informed perspective from someone who can articulate issues that may not be raised because of the too-often-myopic nature of academicians. Also, the perspective she gains from discussions makes her own assignments and tasks more understandable because of her understanding of the overall context into which they fall. She has taken assumed responsibilities as grants coordinator for the division and Independent Colleges Office liaison for the institution. She is also the staff representative on the executive committee for the planning and construction effort for the science building. These roles have provided flexible room for her own professional growth, new leadership opportunities within the division and institution as a whole, and a new synergism of interaction with the dean and the faculty that makes her integral to, rather than a servant of, the program as a whole.

Securing Essential Resources

Another venue for activity at the dean's level is ensuring that the physical infrastructure for the division is adequate and serves students and faculty well. There is a cost for instrumentation that must be met continually if we are to provide students with the best opportunities for learning possible. At the institutional level, Hope College provides generous but insufficient capital equipment funds. However, faculty interested in seeking equipment, particularly through the National Science Foundation (NSF) programs for instructional laboratory improvement, have tangible support from the institutional budget line item for grant-matching funds. They are encouraged even more strongly because the institution makes a commitment to fund proposals that are not successful with external agencies.

The key to our success is the willingness of faculty and administrators to continually seek funds from outside the institution for programs and research. Faculty are rewarded for this in different ways. The most immediate benefit is from having to think through the needs and goals of a project about which he or she is passionate and for engaging campus colleagues in the development of a competitive proposal. Then comes the value of having responses from the review panel, whether or not the grant is awarded. Persistent involvement in authoring proposals is an expectation of the entire division, and this expectation is one reason that our faculty has achieved significant success in this regard over the years. As dean, I recognize the point of submitting a proposal, thanking faculty for their hard work with a pat on the back, a smile, and a modest gift of flowers, wine, dinner, or something particularly appropriate for that individual or writing team. Goodwill and enthusiasm prevail, and resources are found. Over the past five years, grant awards to faculty in science and mathematics in our division have averaged $1.5 million a year, which includes over $400,000 annually from NSF.

We also recognize that outside funds cannot be expected to be the sole source of support to enhance and enrich our programs. To that end, an endowment fund of $1.4 million has been developed to provide income to the dean to use within the division. The dean also has a reasonable annual budget (about $50,000) with which to work to promote divisional activities not covered by individual department budgets (each department has an individual budget ranging from a low of $20,000 annually [mathematics] through a high of $160,000 annually [chemistry]). Thus, the cost in dollars for running our program, while high, is not as high as the cost in commitment—a cost that is intangible in value.

Conclusion

The science dean is thus expected to be a campus and divisional leader, is expected to help faculty to frame programs that best suit institutional and disciplinary needs, and is the key advocate for programs both inside and external to the institution. The record of activity in this role over the years at Hope College suggests this as a model for institutions seeking to build a similar culture on their campus.

JAMES M. GENTILE is dean for the natural sciences at Hope College, Holland, Michigan.

17

A president reviews the critical elements of a capital campaign program.

Fund Development for Science Facilities

James R. Appleton

While some might argue that there are unique features in fund development for science facilities, I prefer to think about how to apply the basics of all fund development to this particular set of objectives. Therefore, I suggest that these ideas for presidents and other academic leaders to consider when launching a program to secure funding for a capital project for the sciences apply to all major funding objectives, although my examples and applications fit the sciences.

The experience that one brings to the table when discussing fund development is not always clear. I have assumed that the president reading this chapter may be a bit new to this part of his or her executive responsibilities and has not had much direct experience in fund development. Perhaps some more experienced readers may also gain from these considerations. Most of us have learned the trade by engaging directly in this aspect of our work with a bit of trial and error as we apply our leadership style and skills. Few of us are called on more than once in a presidential career to undertake a major campaign for new spaces for science.

The president must be fully engaged in a project of this magnitude and importance to the campus. The faculty will expect it, and major donor prospects will assume it. The professional personnel and faculty deserve this full attention and leadership. Such a science capital project may be one of the most expensive fund development projects ever mounted on a campus. And because it will make a significant impact on the educational landscape of the institution for years to come, the time and attention will be well rewarded.

At the front end of the project, the president may need to come to understand the extent and limitations of the current science programs, the pedagogy, the scholarly agenda of faculty, the areas of distinction on which the institution might build, and the potential to be realized with improved spaces for teaching and research. Becoming science savvy will ensure that the president has the necessary grounding to exercise the role of broker at the campus level as competing interests surface, as well as the role of advocate both internally and externally to secure the resources needed to realize this project.

One should not overlook the importance of what might be called cheer-leading. A major facilities project such as this, from the point of imagining it to realizing it, will add to the work load of faculty and administrative leaders. Even those who are excited about the project and whose scholarly work will be enhanced by it need encouragement. Fund development officers and business personnel also need to be encouraged. Seeking gifts and grants can at times be tedious; business officers will have to determine how the increased space will be managed and how to keep the lights on (that is, how to pay the bills to do so). And the process will not flow at an even pace. The president can and must develop approaches consistent with his or her leadership style to encourage, cajole, excite, and reward effective and creative achievements and accomplishments.

No Academic Plan, No Program

The first step, obvious but essential, is to ensure that the academic mission and institutional objectives to be realized by this science project are clearly understood and articulated. It may appear that this step in the process is not actually part of fund development. However, it must at least be viewed as a precursor to the actual tasks for securing the resources required. It is essential that adequate time and attention be given to establishing a clear agenda for the science facilities to be built. This might take not just months but years, depending on the status of the programs to be accommodated in these facilities. This is the most critical part of the process, and the president must both step back and let faculty work things out and keep actively involved so that they stay focused and committed, with high morale.

It begins with the faculty and academic leadership assessing the academic programs themselves. This step involves an iterative process among faculty, academic leadership, and sometimes the office of the president. It eventually engages an architect meeting with all parties concerned. This will result in a concept paper about the value of these programs and the need for the facilities. This should lead to engaging business personnel, academic leadership, and especially the president to settling on a scope of work for the project and setting a clear expectation regarding cost.

By way of example, the University of Redlands took five years, from 1990 to 1995, to build the case for a $33 million science and math complex.

Through this process, we established a bold objective: to place the university in the forefront of undergraduate science and mathematics education. The story began with a self-study by faculty, the engagement of consultants, visits to other institutions, and involvement with Project Kaleidoscope. The process continued with major reforms in curriculum, authorization for additional faculty positions, an increase in equipment and technology budgets, and finally the development of a plan that could be translated into space needs. Were these steps not completed in sequence, success in fund development could not have been assured.

Early in the process, the president, or in larger institutions the appropriate executive representing the president, must set clear limits on the project cost. The president can take two possible actions regarding cost:

Establish a tentative scope of the project, move through construction drawings, urge restraint, but decide that if the estimate of cost exceeds the original projection once construction drawings are complete, the entire project will be built regardless of cost. This may be more appropriate in a renovation when surprises are bound to arise, and one might build considerable contingency into that project.

Set an outside limit to cost and insist that the project be tailored to fit that box.

I strongly urge that the president adopt the second course of action unless there is an unlimited budget.

Be Able to Articulate the Case Equally for the Institution and the Project

Three essential questions must be answered at the outset. They are simple, yet the answers that make sense to the potential donors and the academic elite are complex:

- Why is this project important?
- Why at this university or college?
- How does this project add distinction to my institution?

The answers to these questions must be articulated with specifics, not generalities, and the answers must be compelling. The message must ring with the notion that the college or university cannot flourish (maybe even survive) without support for this project. Trustees, executive leaders, faculty, and volunteers must have the documentation that enables them to describe their love affair with the institution and convince that the project is more important than anything else on the horizon. Persons or foundations with funds to invest must understand why they should place their resources with this institution and this project rather than with other options.

Engage Faculty and Academic Leadership

The president should be intentional in ensuring that all development officers recognize how valuable faculty and academic leaders can be at appropriate junctures in the forthcoming process. Who better than faculty to
represent the case for the programs to be housed in new or renovated facilities? Who is more passionate for their work than faculty who will benefit
from the spaces? Faculty's work is reflected in the specific programs, and
the facilities provide the spaces for the programs to be housed. The pride
of the faculty in their own work, this program, and the institution will carry
the day. Faculty might also include students in this process to detail their
academic progress or display their undergraduate research to a symposium
in which potential donors participate. The enthusiasm of students can be
infectious.

If key faculty and academic administrative leaders are engaged in the
process from the outset, and therefore understand the compromises that
find their way into any facility project, they also can be called on to help
deal with the competing pressures and resulting need for balancing expectations with realities. At the University of Redlands, a project team was
developed that included the vice president for university relations, the director of fund development, the director of physical plant, the physical plant
construction supervisor, the director of the science and mathematics center, a senior chemistry faculty member, and a consultant. This group was
engaged at all stages of the project and in all important policy decisions.

Some discussion with faculty by academic leadership or development
staff may be useful prior to a campus visit by a foundation program director or other donor prospects. The faculty and the president deserve the same
briefings and advice when meeting with donor prospects. Ideas about how
to match a university's needs with donors' interests will be an important part
of this primer.

Faculty and academic leadership can be helpful after the project is
complete by communicating to donors the benefits of the facility. This
is part of good stewardship. Faculty at the University of Redlands volun-
teered to send updates to science center major donors about the progress
being made and the benefits to students. They also hosted donors at the
groundbreaking and dedication ceremonies. The positive feedback from
these donors was gratifying.

Cues About the Stages of Fund Development

One of my mentors, Roger Olsen, then senior vice president at the
University of Southern California, helped me see that there is a definite
sequence to successful interaction with persons or foundations to further
fund development:

1. *Identify the persons or foundations with the capability to give who might fund portions of this project if motivated.* To illustrate, from a list of science graduates over a number of years, faculty can be asked to identify graduates they know. Selected graduates may be in industries or in science or technology professions that suggest they might be inclined to support science. From a review of foundations, the list can be built of those who will have interest in the institution and perhaps special interests in projects like this. At the University of Redlands, one graduate identified by a long-time faculty member helped us lead a mini-campaign among a small group of his alumni friends to fund a laboratory in honor of a deceased and revered faculty member.

2. *Evaluate their potential.* How much might they give, under what conditions, and what might create the largest support? These are key questions to be answered that might require conversations with others, review of published materials, a formal feasibility study, or a series of conversations.

3. *Cultivate their interest.* Do not consider this to be manipulative; everything should be done with integrity and with the best interests in mind for the individual or foundation and the university or college. Major donor prospects should visit the existing labs if possible; the needs will be obvious. Visiting another campus with a donor prospect where instrumentation exists that is similar to that to be included in your project might help seal the deal.

4. *Solicit.* Ultimately, someone must make the ask. The person making this request must be highly regarded by the donor. It is commonly understood that individuals and foundations give to institutions where the personnel are respected and trusted.

5. *Engage in stewardship.* Donors are important. Do not make the mistake of disconnecting from the donor after the gift. The individual or foundation has made an investment and deserves to have updates on the value of that investment. Moreover, this communication puts your university or college in good stead with the best prospective donors: current donors.

The order of this sequence to successful fund development is important, and no steps can be overlooked or given only cursory treatment. The president must communicate this sequence to staff managing the process and ensure that they understand it. There is nothing mystical about this— just hard work, disciplined by timetables and clear assignments.

There are a few other cues that might be helpful. One is the importance of developing a strong communication plan. Projects such as a new complex for science, a new building, or a major renovation to house these important programs have a natural consistency, and communicating with this constituency must begin months before the other stages of fund development are launched. A full year prior to the start of our A Place for Science campaign at the University of Redlands, the public relations officers wrote a variety of science-related stories for the alumni magazine. This was to begin to plant the seed for a constituency well informed about our needs and our dreams. To introduce the campaign to those alumni with a degree in one of the fields of science or engineering and to specific foundations as well, a brochure describing the project was developed. As with all other campaign-related activities, this was done in close coordination with the faculty and others involved with the project. The initial brochure took the form of a glossy newsletter and was followed by several other newsletters in a similar format. Our aim was to keep these groups informed about and interested in our project. The final newsletter was a joy to produce: the honor roll call of donors.

The best fund development campaign is to be able to complete the entire project with one gift, the second best campaign is two gifts to completion, and the third best is three gifts. Major gifts must be secured up front in order to motivate smaller donors to believe in the project. Preferably, a quiet phase in the early stages of fund development will focus on the largest donor prospects so that once the public is aware of the campaign, it is well on the way to completion.

Show that the president is engaged in the process. Some donors, and especially foundations, expect the president to be highly involved in the project. It is useful to have a single senior fund development professional assigned to manage and coordinate all aspects of fund development for the specific project. Ideally, this person would also have been engaged as an observer in the process from the beginning, including the academic planning phases. Each prospective donor should have a development staff person assigned to him or her and a schedule of deadlines established to cultivate and solicit the donor. This may require weeks, months, or even years. Restructuring the time line should happen deliberately and with design, keeping in mind that there are several reasons that such dates may slip (for example, the prospect is out of town).

I have two final pieces of advice. First, it is good practice to postpone putting the shovel into the ground until the project is fully pledged; and, second, consider adding an increment of endowment funds for equipment upgrades and maintenance of the facility in the fund development goal.

Conclusion

Fund development success must always be credited to a team effort. When the lead gift for, say, $5 million is secured for the project, who is to be applauded? The faculty who will teach and engage in scholarship in the new facilities and have developed the program statement? The academic administrators? Volunteer trustees? The fund development leadership? The president? The foundations and individual donors? What is called for is a group hug that the president must be sure to orchestrate. All parties involved, however removed from the actual solicitation, have played a role in the success of the process.

JAMES R. APPLETON is president of the University of Redlands, Redlands, California.

18

How people are drawn into and engaged with the process of planning new facilities for science has a direct relationship with the quality and character of the spaces that emerge from that effort.

The People and Process of Investing in Facilities

Elizabeth S. Boylan

Recently while preparing for a presentation and discussion with our trustees regarding Barnard College's capital building needs, I came across the well-known Winston Churchill quotation that captures my experience: "We shape buildings. Thereafter they shape us." It points to the profound influence that work space has on the workplace, that is, on our human capital and their surroundings. Therefore, those who have a hand in renovating or planning new facilities must do so with utmost care. It is critical to pay attention to the best prevailing wisdom as to how buildings and interior spaces can contribute to the potential people have—to their interactions, creativity, productivity, and capacity to learn.

I have been asked to give my perspective, based on my experience, on how to make the best investment in the facilities used by students and faculty in the sciences: how to establish working relationships, set expectations, and involve the various constituencies to get the most from the investment in facilities for teaching and research in science.

I have a caveat to trustees, presidents, provosts, and deans who are not themselves scientists: if there is in all of us a territorial imperative and a propensity to be consumed by actual or perceived deficiencies with regard to assigned space, such imperatives and propensities are taken to higher orders of magnitude by those in facility-dependent fields such as (but not exclusively) the laboratory sciences. Bright and even lighting, plenty of electrical power, reliable building services and temperature regulation, efficient use of space, and more are high stakes to those whose work depends on the building environment. Do not assume the architects will know everything they need to know about the particularities of the kinds of teaching and research done at the present and planned for the future. Do not assume the faculty and staff know what they will need or what the options are. Do enough research so that you know the questions to ask and how to maximize the likelihood that the building or renovation will achieve its fullest potential.

I have been party to some building projects that have gone smoothly and have come in under budget; they have been few, but they have been enough in number to keep me optimistic that it can be done. Other projects have had devilish lives of their own, and it is hard to figure how many things can go wrong at once or in quick succession, or both. Twenty-twenty hindsight on the good and the bad has allowed me to come up with some working principles that appear to lead toward more satisfactory and satisfying outcomes (though not even the best of plans, planners, architects, and construction folks ensures against things going awry).

Here are some thoughts on the process from the point before the architects are selected to during and after moving in; they are lessons learned, some the hard way, written for deans, provosts, and presidents who have building projects on the horizon. Attention to these people and process factors is as important in the long run as having the land or space, dreaming the dream, raising the money, and giving the final okay to proceed.

1. *Involve faculty in the architect selection process.* A great deal is at stake in defining the scope and character of a project during the architect selection process: what is in the request for proposals and who is chosen. Having key faculty involved from the start contributes to a sense of buy-in, educates (some of) the faculty as to the opportunities and constraints that will be operating, and helps the architect gain a sense of who the end users will be from the beginning.

2. *Insist that the architects and the departments involved talk early and often as plans develop.* Make sure that the architects listen for variations on a theme, reflections of microclimates from department to department that should be preserved—even enhanced—for their individual optimal functioning. One size does not fit all, no matter how aesthetically pleasing and pure (and cost-effective) it may appear. While it is appropriate to force discussion on this issue of departmental autonomy somewhat and avoid truly idiosyncratic (and inflexible) structures, trying to force round pegs into square holes is not the way to go. Churchill was right: space can facilitate activity or deform and inhibit it. If the project is to serve many individuals or groups, attention should be paid up front to making the best matches between user preferences and utilitarian pressures.

3. *Hire competent construction managers who represent the institution's interests in dealing with contractors.* Make sure they know what your institution's interests really are. Have them consult regularly with the faculty and staff who will be occupying the space, so that when changes have to be

made on the spot during construction, they have a good sense as to what would be an acceptable deviation from the plan and what will interfere with or prevent the eventual occupants from doing their best work.

4. *Support the involvement of at least one or a few faculty, and have them be working partners throughout the planning and building process.* It takes time for faculty and staff to learn enough to interpret architectural plans—electrical and lighting diagrams, for example, and placement of plumbing lines. It takes time to go to weekly sessions where problems are identified and decisions are made on acceptable alternatives. One can free up staff to take on these roles, but for big projects, there is a lot to be said for paying faculty—in money or time, or both—to slog through the minutiae and develop the expertise so that they can know firsthand when and why decisions were made and can alert others when seemingly innocuous changes will result in major functional deficits.

5. *Consider carefully how such faculty representatives are selected or appointed and what credibility and standing they have among their peers.* Make sure that the chosen faculty keep in touch with their colleagues as plans and construction proceed. They may be called on to make the case for certain decisions; they may be called to task for their complicity in those decisions.

6. *Prepare the community for change and hardship during the construction process.* Be truly vigilant in preparing for contingencies: communicating broadly what will happen when, how bad and long it will be that way, whom to call if it interferes with planned activity. Ensure that enough serious thought is given to mitigating the effects of noise, dirt, intrusion, and safety and security concerns. Those who will directly gain from the construction will have some greater, but not infinite, acceptance of inconvenience and adversity during the construction. Those who gain little or nothing and still have to be aggravated will have few qualms about expressing their views and airing their gripes. Even a most ardent champion of the building project can be bent into a figure of gloom and doom when apparently random events disrupt work habits, particularly when they detract from the precious time faculty have with their students in class.

7. *Prepare the community for the move-in phase.* Be prepared for loose ends, punch lists that grow out of sight, and people who should be feeling happy and grateful for new facilities but are acting as though the sky had fallen. Change is hard, even when it is for the long-term benefit. No good deed goes unpunished. Prepare to be a sponge, and absorb the frustration, anger, tension, and fatigue that accompany any major move.

8. *Take a vacation.* Do this as soon as there is a certificate of occupancy and the air-handling systems are sufficiently balanced so that human comfort is reasonably assured. Do not stop into an Internet café to check e-mail. Let people feather their new nests, put up family photos and posters, adjust their desk chair heights, sort their new file drawers, figure out the new telephones. Then return for office warmings, and celebrate and toast their good

taste. Acknowledge again their pain and suffering and tolerance during the building process. Praise publicly those who helped make it happen. Pay the bills. Enjoy a fleeting moment or two of private satisfaction.

9. *Dream about what is next.*

ELIZABETH S. BOYLAN is provost and dean of the faculty at Barnard College, New York City.

19

Major curricular or pedagogical change should be launched with a thorough communications plan well in hand.

Communication in Reform

Melvin D. George

"They don't communicate." This is doubtless the most common complaint about administrators and heard from faculty and staff at all sorts of institutions from coast to coast. It is certainly true that this complaint sometimes means something quite different. Not infrequently, it is used as a substitute for, "I do not like what I heard from them." In such cases, the complaint really assumes that "to communicate" means "to communicate a message I approve." Most often, however, the criticism is valid, and the circumstances that led to it were avoidable by carefully considering the variety of constituencies who will believe they should not only have been told what was to happen, but should have been actively consulted about it.

All too often, an administrator about to make a change fails to think through and put in motion a communications plan as an integral prelude to and part of the change. Developing and carrying out such a thoughtful communications plan is important, in particular, if a significant change in pedagogy or curriculum is contemplated. In the process of making such a transformation, there is a lot of communication needed at all stages, with different levels of intensity, and of varying breadth and scope as the process proceeds. I am assuming here that there has been enough preliminary involvement with faculty and other administrators to have led to the formulation of a fairly specific but not yet detailed final proposal. At such a point, a rather formal communications plan becomes essential. And the plan should be in place prior to an actual decision to proceed with change, because once a decision is announced, communications can spin out of control if there is no thoughtful plan for those communications.

Such a plan needs to reflect the particular campus culture and tradition. What the institutional history has been will influence the way people receive the idea being proposed, and the traditions of communication and consultation will play an important role in how messages are heard. Following are some suggestions regarding such a plan, assuming that a well-conceived idea for change has been at least tentatively formulated in a way that will have credibility in the campus community:

1. *Think of communication as a two-way process, not a one-way street.* In beginning to develop a communications plan, remember that communicating involves not only speaking and writing but also listening. Major institutional change is threatening, dislocating, and stressful. Listening to concerns (some of which are actually valid), hearing objections (some of which are substantive), and being willing to shape the final proposal to take these into consideration are important parts of communicating and need to occur sooner rather than later.

2. *Gather data relevant to a final shaping of and making a decision to implement the change.* Part of any successful communications plan is preparing a knowledge base that anticipates questions or criticisms by assembling data or other information in advance. It is hard to be too specific about the data and information needs without knowing the nature of the particular change contemplated. As examples, information should have been collected about the experiences (both processes and outcomes) of similar institutions that have instituted a similar change. There should be plenty of information about student patterns of enrollment, persistence, achievement, and interest. There should be accurate data about faculty workloads, perceptions, and positions now open and anticipated to be open. There should be careful projections of financial needs and implications.

3. *Carefully consider all the people who will be—or who will think they will be—affected by such a change.* Some of these constituencies are crucial to the decision about and successful implementation of a major educational change. Certainly, faculty in affected departments are key. Among the others are faculty, chairs, and deans in user departments; curriculum committees; teaching assistants and lab assistants who may have changed responsibilities; financial officers (including development staff) who will have responsibility for funding the change; and admissions staff who recruit students and provide liaison with high school teachers and faculty. There are others who will certainly feel they should know and perhaps have been consulted: the board of trustees, public relations staff, employers of graduates, student advisory committees, career counseling centers, alumni of affected departments, and donors who have given to the areas affected or have an interest in these departments. Make a comprehensive list, and categorize the groups by the urgency of communication and nature of consultation desirable.

4. *Pay particular attention to faculty in affected departments.* Some may be hostile because they feel their contributions are not being appreciated or that their teaching style or philosophy is being rejected. The various strengths of faculty need to be honored where possible, improved in a

nonjudgmental way if necessary. It may seem too large an investment of time, but there is no substitute for personal conversations with faculty in their offices and laboratories.

5. *Develop a communications plan by making a time line of needs and opportunities for consultation and communication with each of the constituencies who will be affected by the change.* In each case, anticipate questions and objections, and review the data gathered to be reasonably sure there are no potentially embarrassing gaps. Decide who should do the communicating, recognizing that this will probably vary by the audience and the topic. In general, as long as the messages are consistent, it is probably better to have more people rather than fewer involved in the communicating.

6. *Test your tentative plan in three ways.* First, look at an organization chart or telephone directory of offices for your campus. Be sure no important unit has been omitted from the plan; if in doubt, include it. Second, review the plan with all those directly involved in making a decision about whether to proceed. Has anything been left out? Finally, contact a trusted colleague at another institution, preferably one who has undergone a somewhat similar change. Ask that person to critique your plan with you.

These suggestions should help avoid a number of potential pitfalls. But if an unexpected obstacle arises, as it often does, try not to be defensive, admit any mistakes you have made, apologize when necessary, and keep a sense of humor, especially about yourself. Finally, be willing to modify the communications plan itself if you discover a gap or a problem. Just as with the proposed change itself, a modification is not usually a sign of failure but an indication of healthy flexibility and willingness not only to listen but to accept suggestions.

Do not let a good idea founder on the rocks of criticism that there has been inadequate communication. A communications plan will not guarantee success, but the lack of one will certainly make failure much more likely. Be inclusive, be open to the views of others, and be strategic.

MELVIN D. GEORGE is president emeritus and professor emeritus of mathematics at the University of Missouri, Columbia.

20

Effective institutional decision making about budgets, programs, and facilities must be built on the strong foundation of meaningful evaluation.

Assessment to Improve Student Learning

David F. Brakke, Douglas T. Brown

Assessment is a process of ongoing formative and summative evaluation that should be easily understood and embraced for what it can do to improve student learning and the quality of institutions. Results of assessment are the drivers of reform, and thus any efforts to improve student learning must be tied to ongoing evaluation and assessment.

The assessment movement got off to a rocky start; it has unfortunately been viewed suspiciously by many faculty members as not a means of gaining useful information about student attitudes, preconceptions, learning, or understanding but instead as a means of evaluating their scholarly work. Faculty bristle when politicians speak of accountability, fearing intrusions into how the curriculum is designed or delivered.

Faculty understand and appreciate the conceptual basis for assessment, which is something like research in educational practice, even if they might not relate to assessment language, or feel it restricts their academic freedom (a phrase that is often interpreted to mean something well beyond what is intended or reasonable). This unfortunate tie for some faculty to accountability or institutional effectiveness has been confusing and led in many cases to widespread resistance.

But today's environment is more complex than ever before; institutions ignore public calls for accountability at their potential peril. What can we say to parents, students, or the larger public if we do not establish clear goals and examine our progress toward meeting them? The critical questions are:

NEW DIRECTIONS FOR HIGHER EDUCATION, no. 119, Fall 2002 © Wiley Periodicals, Inc.

- How can we better frame and structure the conversation about assessment?
- What should we focus on, and can we determine how assessment should be done and the results used?
- Who needs to know?

For example, politicians have a practical interest in knowing something about outcomes. They may legitimately ask how we document student performance or demonstrate what is accomplished with the investment made in public institutions. Students and parents may wonder why a curriculum is structured in a certain way and ask what the requirements and offerings established by departments and institutions are intended to achieve. They may ask, for example, about the goals of general education programs and how or if they are tied to the university's mission or built on in the major. We should not assume that general education learning objectives are synonymous with what we might expect of graduates. Disciplinary and professional programs for majors should have clearly stated learning outcomes also. Institutions talk about being student centered, but without an explicit definition of what is expected of students and how the student centeredness will be measured, responses to politicians, parents, and students will be unconvincing.

There is significant value in the various forms and approaches of assessment. Faculty need to understand how formative assessment helps document how students' attitudes and conceptual understanding are changing as a result of what they are learning in their courses and labs. Faculty also need to understand that data about impact on student learning can bolster requests to administrators for new programs or more sophisticated instrumentation. Even for such things that many consider valuable, such as undergraduate research experiences, there is yet too little evidence to support assumptions and assertions about the efficacy of this experience. This becomes, at the institutional level, an undertaking that goes beyond the work of an individual faculty member or department. Setting an agenda for formative evaluation that is linked to institutional decision making about budgets, curricular programs must become a campuswide priority.

When this becomes such a priority, then one barrier to faculty awareness and use can be addressed. There are many faculty who recognize a need for assessment conceptually but do not have the background to make use of assessment as a tool. The institutionwide approach also helps move from a negative mind-set in regard to evaluation, recentering the focus on the development of the whole student. This discussion needs to be widespread and include proponents and skeptics alike, along with faculty and staff with experience in quantitative and qualitative assessments so that a more complete assessment of changes—in student attitudes, perceptions, integration of knowledge, and conceptual understanding as a result of their campus experiences in and beyond the classroom—can be realized.

The education of the whole student is perhaps best cast in terms of teaching all students what we expect educated citizens to know, and then quantitative, scientific, and technological literacy or reasoning is our focus. The attention on the skills of citizenship suggests that students leave able to communicate and are facile with technology and quantitative approaches within the disciplines and professional programs. These conversations should recognize the enhancement in the major of skills and competencies that build from general education and represent the overall educational impact.

A workable structure for assessment programs has the following components:

- Moves the focus from teaching to learning, a focus reflected in the performance evaluation of individuals and departments
- Considers goals and measurable outcomes for general education and major programs
- Is based on findings of cognitive research
- Reflects clear institutional purpose and vision for skills and abilities expected of all students
- Gives attention to the cognitive development of the student
- Gives attention to the attitudes and preconceptions of students
- Effectively demonstrates the impact of the teaching practice and other experiences on the learning of students

The assessment of student learning is an effective organizing frame for work in institutions. It also can be an effective way to focus attention on what is most important: the development and learning of students. By building a culture focused on student learning and development, assessment will follow as a direct consequence. Our own curiosity and empirical nature will not let us focus on learning and then fail to attempt to measure how well we might be doing. Resulting from this attention will also be enhanced communication across a campus that is centered on the shared value of student learning.

Assessment could be feared if we worried about what we might learn. But if we had evidence that something was not producing what we wanted, wouldn't we try to make adjustments in our curricula and their delivery? With meaningful assessment, we can build an adaptive curriculum that is responsive to what we learn from the results. In turn, that should produce a campus that becomes a learning organization, capturing information and making effective use of it in continuing to improve.

As assessment becomes part of a culture, and not apart from it, it becomes a collective responsibility to accomplish—one that is translated into action at the individual, departmental, and institutional levels, each informing the other. It must be supported at all levels with meaningful structures, such as teaching and learning centers, and not only recognized but valued in evaluation procedures for individuals, departments, and colleges. We suggest it is therefore necessary to recognize and reward a department for collective accomplishments.

Finally, to see education as a process and learning as the outcome frees us to experiment and find ways to demonstrate our effectiveness. It is remarkable that as scientists and educators, we know so little about how students learn and how we might improve that learning. Even matters we assume to be self-evident, such as undergraduate research experiences, have been typically evaluated on the basis of students going on to graduate degrees and not on the learning process or how their experience resulted in improved critical thinking skills or cognitive development. Assessment of student outcomes can be an effective mechanism resulting in positive and sustained change and improvement in our institutions.

We have much to gain as individuals, departments, and institutions by focusing on what we can learn through effective assessment and very much to lose if we cannot explain to publics and constituents the value of what we do in terms of student learning, development, and the abilities they carry from colleges and universities. Accomplishing this goal will require effective, outward-looking leadership that sees interrelationships and connectivity within an institution and the collective responsibility for educating all students.

DAVID F. BRAKKE *is dean of the College of Science and Mathematics and professor of biology at James Madison University, Harrisonburg, Virginia.*

DOUGLAS T. BROWN *is vice president for academic affairs and professor of psychology at James Madison University.*

INDEX

Academic plan, 72
Accountability, 119
Administrators. *See* Leaders
Albright, M. J., 61, 63
Alstete, J. W., 62
Alverno College, 62
American Association for Higher Education, 60
American Association for the Advancement of Science, 29, 30
Appleton, J. R., 103
Architects, 112
Assessment: and accountability, 119; benefits of, 121; components of, 121; and culture, 121; definition of, 45, 119; and experimentation in learning, 122; of facilities, 72–73; faculty beliefs about, 45, 119; frequency of, 43; for grant proposals, 47–49; importance of, 45; importance of different approaches to, 120; interviews for, 48; and learning and teaching centers, 62; linking to department goals, 67–68; and program development, 46–49; questionnaires for, 48; recognition tests for, 42, 43; reform of, 62; of return on faculty costs, 56–58. *See also* Evaluation
Association of American Colleges and Universities, 60
Audience, campus plan, 75
Audit, facility, 72–73
Austin, A. E., 62, 63

Barnard College, 111
Bell Labs, 25
Benchmarking, 18–19
Benchmarks. *See* Standards
Benchmarks for Science Literacy, 30
Blue-collar workers, 10
Boice, R., 61, 62
Bowdoin College, 45–49
Boyer, E., 65
Boylan, E. S., 111
Brady, T. E., 37
Brakke, D. F., 119
Brown, D. T., 119

Bush Foundation, 60
Bush, V., 11

Cambridge Technology Partners, 83
Campbell, G., Jr., 23
Campus planning, 70–76
Career counseling, 67
Career opportunities, 1
Carleton College, 60
Center for Research on Learning and Teaching (University of Michigan), 59
Center for Teaching Excellence (University of Kansas), 59
Center for Teaching, Learning, and Writing (Duke University), 61
Churchill, W., 111
Circles of Learning for Entering Students, 38–39
Cognitive psychology, 41–43
Collaborations: among faculty and architects, 112, 113; among faculty and leaders for reform, 88–89; among K–16 schools, 7–9; among science dean and faculty, 97–98; in campus planning, 74; emergence of, 19; for faculty funding, 56; goals of, 29; learning and teaching centers for, 60, 61; for minority students' success, 37–39
College: The Undergraduate Experience in America, 65
Collegis, 78
Communication: with community regarding new facility, 113; with donors, 107–108; guidelines for, 116–117; importance of, 115; lack of, 115; plan for, 115–117; as two-way process, 116
Community, effect of new facility on, 113
Conover, K., 4
Construction managers, 112–113
Costs: of facilities, 70–71; of faculty, 53–54, 55, 99; fixed asset, 53–54; of math programs, 90, 91; nonfixed asset, 54, 55; of science programs, 90, 91; setting limits to, 105; of tenure, 53; of undergraduat programs, 89–90
Cote, C. B., 45

123

Graphics, campus plan, 75
Graves, B., 78, 79
Graves,W., 83
Grouping: of minority students, 26; research on, 26
Grouping students, 26

Halpern, D. F., 41
Harvard, 60
Haynes, J. K., 65
Heterick, R., 83
Heterogeneous grouping, 26
Hill, S., 27
Hutchings, P., 61
Hybrid learning, 79

Inner-city students, 24
Institutional plan, 72, 95
Intelligence, 25–27
Interviews, 48

Johnson, D. K., 62
Jordan, M., 45
Jordan, T., 33

K–12 teachers, 1, 17, 30
Kentucky Community and Technical College System, 83
Kentucky Virtual University, 83

La Nasa, S. M., 62
Laboratory experiences, 34, 35, 39, 42–43
Leaders: benchmarking of, 18–19; engagement of, 103, 106, 108; involvement of, 19; motivation of, 104; partnering with faculty for reform, 88–89; responsibility for student learning, 11; science dean as, 97–101; science knowledge of, 104
Learning: and complex thinking, 17–18; definition of, 16; depth of, 31; effect of facilities on, 89, 111; e-learning for, 77–83; experimentation in, 122; hybrid, 79; knowledge of, 17, 41–43; laboratory experiences for, 34, 35, 42–43; leaders' responsibility for, 11; on-line, 79; philosophy of, 41; relationship to environment, 11, 16; research in place of, 10; research on, 31; theories of, 41; Web displayed, 79; Web enhanced, 79
Learning and teaching centers (LTC), 59–63

Learning environment: discovery-based, 2, 16; laboratory experiences in, 34, 35; lectures in, 42; relationship to learning, 11, 16; research in, 16; role of faculty in, 16–17; strengthening of, 3
Lectures, 42
Lidsky, A. J., 69
Listening, 116
LTC. See Learning and teaching centers (LTC)

MacLeish, A., 5
Making a Place for the New American Scholar, 63
Math programs: cost of, 90, 91; need for, 2–3, 15; student enrollment in, 25
Mathematics: career opportunities in, 1; courses for nonmath majors, 34; impact on economic development, 24; lack of knowledge in, 33; language of, 15–16; number of minority students with degrees in, 27; in society, 33
McArthur, D., 77
Mentors, 67
Mission: alignment of department and college, 65–66; development of, 65, 66; discussion of, 66; example of, 66–67; and facility funding, 104–105; importance of, 72; in institutional plan, 72; need for new, 12–13; of undergraduate programs, 2
Morehouse College, 65–68
Morse Academic Plan, 34–35
Morse, S.F.B., 34
Motivation, 104
Mullin, R., 62

Narum, J. L., 5
National Council of Teachers of Mathematics, 30
National Institutes of Health, 39
National Research Council, 30, 33
National Science and Technology Council, 27
National Science Board, 25
National Science Digital Library, 19
National Science Education Standards, 30
National Science Foundation, 11, 19, 39, 100
Nelson, G. D., 29
Networking services, 83
New York University, 33–35

Back Issue/Subscription Order Form

Copy or detach and send to:

Jossey-Bass, A Wiley Company, 989 Market Street, San Francisco CA 94103-1741

Call or fax toll-free: Phone 888-378-2537 6AM-5PM PST; Fax 888-481-2665

Back issues: Please send me the following issues at $27 each

(Important: please include series initials and issue number, such as HE114)

1. HE _____

_____

_____

$ _____Total for single issues

$ _____SHIPPING CHARGES: SURFACE

	Domestic	Canadian
First Item	$5.00	$6.00
Each Add'l Item	$3.00	$1.50

For next-day and second-day delivery rates, call the number listed above.

Subscriptions: Please ❑ start ❑ renew my subscription to *New Directions for Higher Education* for the year 2____ at the following rate:

U.S.	❑ Individual $60	❑ Institutional $131
Canada	❑ Individual $60	❑ Institutional $171
All Others	❑ Individual $84	❑ Institutional $205

$ _____Total single issues and subscriptions (Add appropriate sales tax for your state for single issue orders. No sales tax for U.S. subscriptions. Canadian residents, add GST for subscriptions and single issues.)

Federal Tax ID 135593032   GST 89102 8052

❑ Payment enclosed (U.S. check or money order only)

❑ VISA, MC, AmEx, Discover Card # _____ Exp. date_____

Signature _____ Day phone _____

❑ Bill me (U.S. institutional orders only. Purchase order required)

Purchase order #_____

Name _____

Address _____

_____

Phone_____ E-mail _____

For more information about Jossey-Bass, visit our Web site at: www.josseybass.com

PROMOTION CODE = ND3

HE113 How Accreditation Influences Assessment
James L. Ratcliff, Edward S. Lubinescu, Maureen A. Gaffney
Examples of working programs include new methods of distance-education
program assessment, an institutional accreditation self-study at the
University of Vermont, and the Urban Universities Portfolio Project.
ISBN: 0-7879-5436-5

HE112 Understanding the Role of Public Policy Centers and Institutes in
Fostering University-Government Partnerships
Lynn H. Leverty, David R. Colburn
Examines innovative approaches to developing the structure of programs in
both traditional academic environments and in applied research and
training; attracting and rewarding faculty engaged in public service; and
determining which policy issues to approach at institutional levels.
ISBN: 0-7879-5556-6

HE111 Understanding the Work and Career Paths of Midlevel Administrators
Linda K. Johnsrud, Vicki J. Rosser
Provides information to help institutions develop recruitment efforts to fill
midlevel administration positions and enlighten individuals about career
possibilities in midlevel administration.
ISBN: 0-7879-5435-7

HE110 Moving Beyond the Gap Between Research and Practice in Higher Education
Adrianna Kezar, Peter Eckel
Provides suggestions for overcoming the research-practice dichotomy, such
as creating a learning community that involves all the stakeholders, and
using campus reading groups to help practitioners engage with scholarship.
ISBN: 0-7879-5434-9

HE109 Involving Commuter Students in Learning
Barbara Jacoby
Provides ways to create communities that meet the needs of students who
live off-campus—from building a sense of community within individual
courses to the creative use physical space, information technology, living-
learning communities, and experiential education programs.
ISBN: 0-7879-5340-7

HE108 Promising Practices in Recruitment, Remediation, and Retention
Gerald H. Gaither
Identifies the best practices for recruitment, remediation, and retention,
describing lessons learned from innovative and successful programs across
the nation, and shows how to adapt these efforts to today's diverse
populations and technological possibilities.
ISBN: 0-7879-4860-8

HE107 Roles and Responsibilities of the Chief Financial Officer
Lucie Lapovsky, Mary P. McKeoan-Moak
Offers strategies for balancing the operating and capital budgets,
maximizing net enrollment revenues, containing costs, planning for the
resource needs of technology, identifying and managing risks, and
investing the endowment wisely.
ISBN: 0-7879-4859-4

Identifies the institutional patterns and support structures that enhance the dissertation process, and describes how the introduction of dissertation-stage financial support and workshops can quicken completion rates.
ISBN: 0-7879-9889-3

HE98   **The Professional School Dean: Meeting the Leadership Challenges**
Michael J. Austin, Frederick L. Ahearn, Richard A. English
Focuses on the demanding leadership roles assumed by deans of social work, law, engineering, nursing, and divinity, providing case illustrations that illuminate the deanship experience at other professional schools.
ISBN: 0-7879-9849-4

HE97   **The University's Role in Economic Development: From Research to Outreach**
James P. Pappas
Offers models the academy can use to foster the ability to harness the research and educational resources of higher education institutions as well as the potential of state and land-grant universities to provide direct services for local and regional economic development through outreach missions.
ISBN: 0-7879-9890-7

HE96   **Preparing Competent College Graduates: Setting New and Higher Expectations for Student Learning**
Elizabeth A. Jones
Using the results of a nationwide study, this volume identifies specific ways institutions can help undergraduates attain the advanced thinking, communication, and problem-solving skills needed in today's society and workplace.
ISBN: 0-7879-9823-0

HE95   **An Administrator's Guide for Responding to Campus Crime: From Prevention to Liability**
Richard Fossey, Michael Clay Smith
Provides advice on crime prevention programs, campus police training, rape prevention, fraud in federal grant programs, and the problems associated with admitting students with criminal backgrounds.
ISBN: 0-7879-9873-7

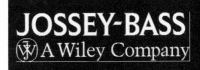